12 Shining Lanterns

Acknowledgements

I would like to give thanks and appreciation to my mother Hazel Humble for her strong faith and support, my daughter Hannah Stronach for being herself and my partner Neal Kydd.

I would also like to thank David Wells for soul guidance and
my teachers Jenni and Sandy.

Revised third edition - September 2019
ISBN-978-1-9164087-2-2
Publisher: The Academy of I (org. 352670)

Publisher: Createspace; 2 edition (January 25, 2018) ,109 pages
Publisher: CreateSpace; 1 edition (December 17, 2016), 82 pages

Contents

Introduction

Welcome to the 12 Shining Lanterns. In presenting a different entry point into Astrology, I felt the need to take astrology back to its roots, by bringing the focus back to nature. To do this I have constructed the lantern wheel of the year. This enables many of the deeper aspects of tropical astrology to be understood by both beginners and advanced students alike, without the need for intense academic study.

The 12 Shining Lanterns connect us to the seasons and the force of the sun - capturing the early origins of Astrology. It is a path of discovery and experience where you will journey with the sun through the 12 signs of the tropical zodiac. The signs and symbols will be easily recognised by their common names and icons which appear in our daily newspapers.

I have organised this book into sections. For people new to the subject I suggest you work your way through the building blocks in section one. They naturally follow through to each individual Lantern. This section is the groundwork to understanding the journey of the sun, the elements and the seasonal influences.

The journey of the lanterns is to complete a study of the Astrological year; lighting the essence of each sign within you - accumulating knowledge and wider self understanding. You may also gain clarity and insight into the motivations and the potential of others.

This book covers the natural paths and correspondences of the zodiac and also depicts its place within the Tree of Life. Many elements in both nature and our own history connect us firmly to Astrology. If you are well versed in these subjects you can move directly into the lantern exercises, meditations and self discovery. It is important to follow the annual progression of the sun, journeying through all the seasons, to finish the complete cycle. The last section contains reference guides and glossaries.

Nature is our greatest learning and via ancient processes and analogy, a journey of self discovery unfolds. By understanding the natural order of the solar year we can bring ourselves into balance and widen our own skills, tolerance and understanding of the ways of others.

What are the 12 Shining Lanterns?

The Lanterns are the essential components of astrology distilled to capture an essence, a potent force you can work with and recognise throughout your life. You will discover how the essences of the 12 lanterns shine within you. By working through each of the lantern exercises you will be able to tap into their energy and engage on a personal level.

As you become aware of the cycles and patterns of the universe, understanding the lanterns gives you the tools to align with nature and in turn connect with your inner nature. Astrology harmonises us with the celestial spheres and attunes us to the keys held in natural law.

Chrysippus tells us: *'This is the very thing that makes up the virtue of the happy person and a well flowing life, when the affairs in life are in every way tuned to the harmony between the individual divine Spirit and the will of the Director of the universe.'*

The Lantern Wheel
Lanterns are shown around the edge of the wheel
aligned with the corresponding
sign and element.

The Lanterns show you what is unique about you - they reveal the real you and allow you to embrace your own creativity and your own internal spark.

'Be yourself; everyone else is already taken' - Oscar Wilde

We are made up of not just one lantern but have within us the framework of all 12 and this template can be used to assist us throughout our whole life. The key is to identify how we react and respond to each influence, so that when we are confronted with that influence, we understand what it triggers within, assisting us to be able to maintain our own space and not lose our energy or our power.

Extract from the **Leo Lantern of Creativity***:* - 'When one knows oneself and understands the inner forces, they do not seek to place blame on others, but instead take responsibility for themselves; using the inner furnace to light the Lantern and illuminate the path ahead. In doing so they also light the way for others, that they may find their own internal light and in turn do the same.'

We light our own lanterns within by working with nature's laws - just like the mutable quality *(explained on page 16)* – where we gather the knowledge and resources required. After which we light the lantern by using our cardinal spark - forged from contemplating the essence of the sign and learning how it operates and shines throughout our life. Lastly, like the fixed quality, we work to anchor the lantern within, so it stays alight. We begin the voyage by reading the information and completing the exercises.   Returning to the lantern wheel, when the need arises, to readjust our inner balance.

For instance; a person with a strong Taurus would feel at home when the light of the sun was harmonising with his nature in May but when the sun reaches its height, he may become hot headed and throw a tantrum as he would feel uncomfortable. Working with the lantern that corresponds with the imbalance or irritation can create an understanding of those forces within and how they are operating. Once he feels at home with them, understands their nature then they are not an alien experience anymore. He will be equipped to deal with those forces in the future.

The wheel of the Zodiac from the mosaic floor of the 6th century synagogue at Beth-Alpha displaying the Sun God Helios in the centre, whom presided over the measurement and divisions of the day, the year and the seasons.

The linking of the Lanterns to the signs, seasonal changes and the path of the sun make up our study of the solar year. The following brief descriptions can be used as an easy look up guide for future reference. We begin our journey at the Spring Equinox with Aries - the Lantern of Energy. Every 30 days the sun moves into a different sign, ending at Pisces, the Lantern of Imagination, as it prepares for the cycle to begin again.

Aries, birth of colourful spring

Urge to survive, the Lantern of Energy, innocence, to pioneer, conquer, spark and motivate action.

Taurus, fertile soil

Urge to manifest, the Lantern of Strength, to sustain, to be patient, determined, practical, abundant and enduring.

Gemini, light warm breezes

Urge to communicate, the Lantern of Language, to think with clarity, socialise, uniting communities, bridging gaps.

Cancer, rock pools and shallow rivers

Urge to respond, the Lantern of Nurturing, to be nourishing, caring, yet industrious, commanding and resilient.

Leo, radiating heat of the sun

Urge to live, the Lantern of Creativity, to lead,
protect, to be confident, loyal, proud and benevolent.

Virgo, tree with strong roots penetrating the earth, branches reaching for heaven

Urge to serve, the Lantern of Reason, perfect techniques,
analyse, reliability, common sense and spiritual beacon.

Libra, autumn leaves blowing in the wind

Urge to love, the Lantern of Beauty, equilibrium, diplomatic,
refined, graceful, peaceful with a sense of justice.

Scorpio, iceberg, frozen water with hidden mass below the surface

Urge to transform, the Lantern of Regeneration, resourceful,
secretive, dynamic, fixed, observant, magnetic and mysterious.

Sagittarius, wild bush fire

Urge to grow, the Lantern of Vision, adventurous, cultural, optimistic, goal driven, idealistic and spontaneous.

Capricorn, cold mountain rocks of earth

Urge to control, the Lantern of Self-Discipline, ambition, to take responsibility for ourselves, nature, our environment and reputation.

Aquarius, ice cold winds

Urge to change, the Lantern of Freedom gained through the restriction of January. To challenge outdated ideas, seek the truth and enlightenment, to be connected to all humanity.

Pisces, wild seas, fathomless depths

Urge to dream, the Lantern of the Imagination, nature sleeps to make way for rebirth, to be empathic, sensitive and wise, experience creates understanding.

The Way of Manifestation

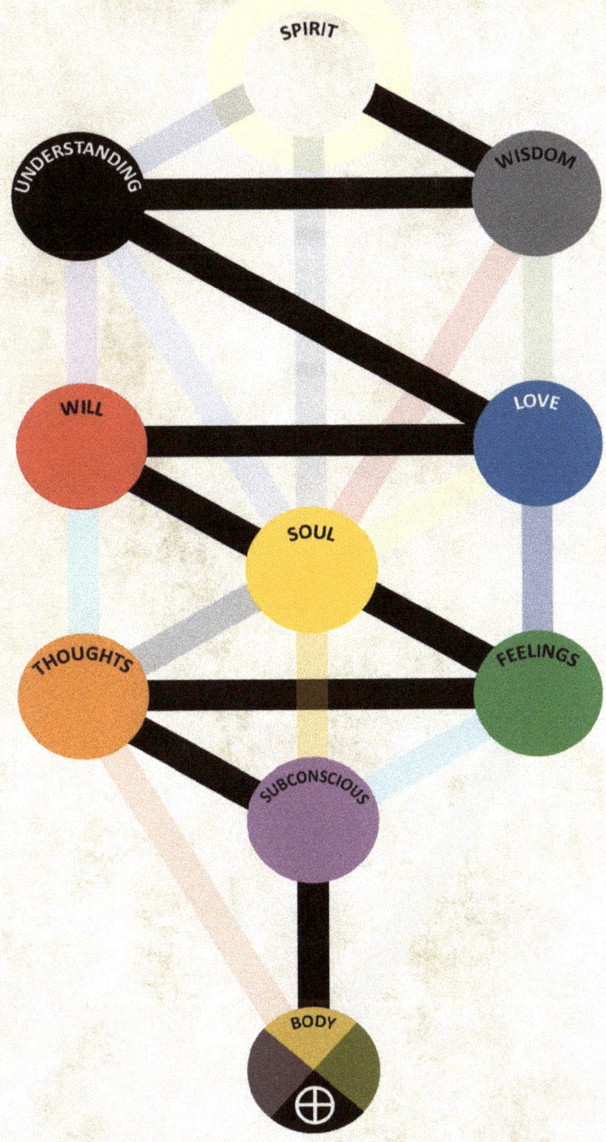

At this point let us connect with the idea that we are essentially spiritual beings operating through our physical body. Understanding nature's cycles can key us into our senses, the environment - the forces around and within us. When this happens it is easier to be aware of that which is in our control and that which is not. Before we proceed with section one - let us firstly consider the map of the Tree of Life.

This map shows the way of descent from our Spiritual essence down through to our body. This map contains many correspondences shown usually as symbols - our subconscious mind recognises and responds to symbols providing a way of communicating to our higher selves. In this book, the illustration of the tree is the Qabalistic Tree of Life and the 12 Shining Lanterns are the zodiac signs.

Section One
Astrology and Nature

The Way of the Sun
Through the ecliptic

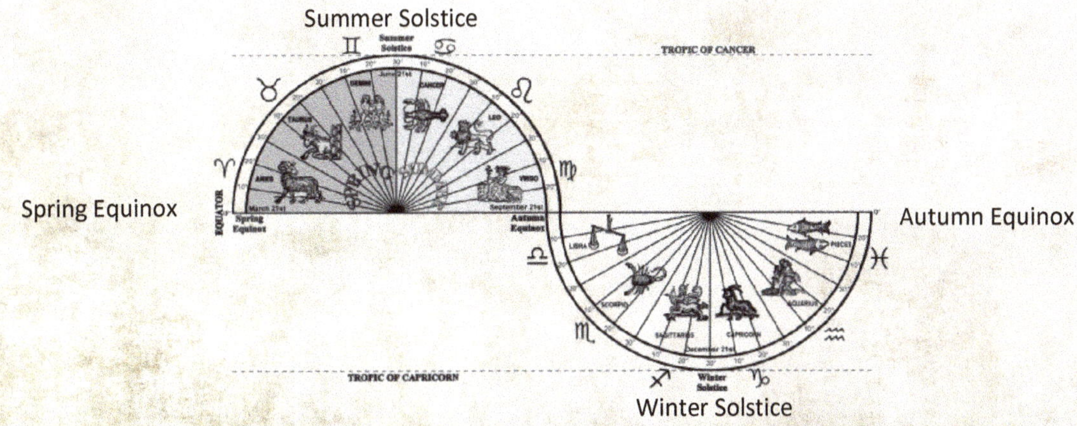

The fundamental building block in Astrology is in the understanding of the sun's journey through the ecliptic belt. The Spring Equinox always occurs on 21st March, the point at 0.0 degree Aries where the Sun begins his yearly journey through the ecliptic. The other signs follow through in 30 degree segments *(known as the 'fixed firmament')* - Cancer is on the 21st June, the date of the Summer Solstice, Libra is always at the Autumn Equinox and the sun enters Capricorn at the Winter Solstice. This pattern above sits between the Tropic of Cancer and the Tropic of Capricorn - known as 'The Sinewave.'

To form the wheel of 12 below, the lower part of the sinewave is placed underneath the upper half, creating the circle. The upper part shows the sun´s journey through the 6 months of Spring and Summer and the lower part shows its journey through the 6 months of Autumn and Winter. We can use this wheel to explain many of Nature's cycles.

Each month has individual qualities that are psychologically married to that time of year and because of this, certain months share an underlying theme.   The four key dates of seasonal change are recognised in the celebration of the Equinoxes and Solstices.

Below we can see an example of how time is plotted on the wheel. The sun rises in the east every morning and sets in the west at dusk. It is at its height when it reaches midday and at its lowest when it reaches midnight. As the sun's light fades from view, the moon's light can then be seen.

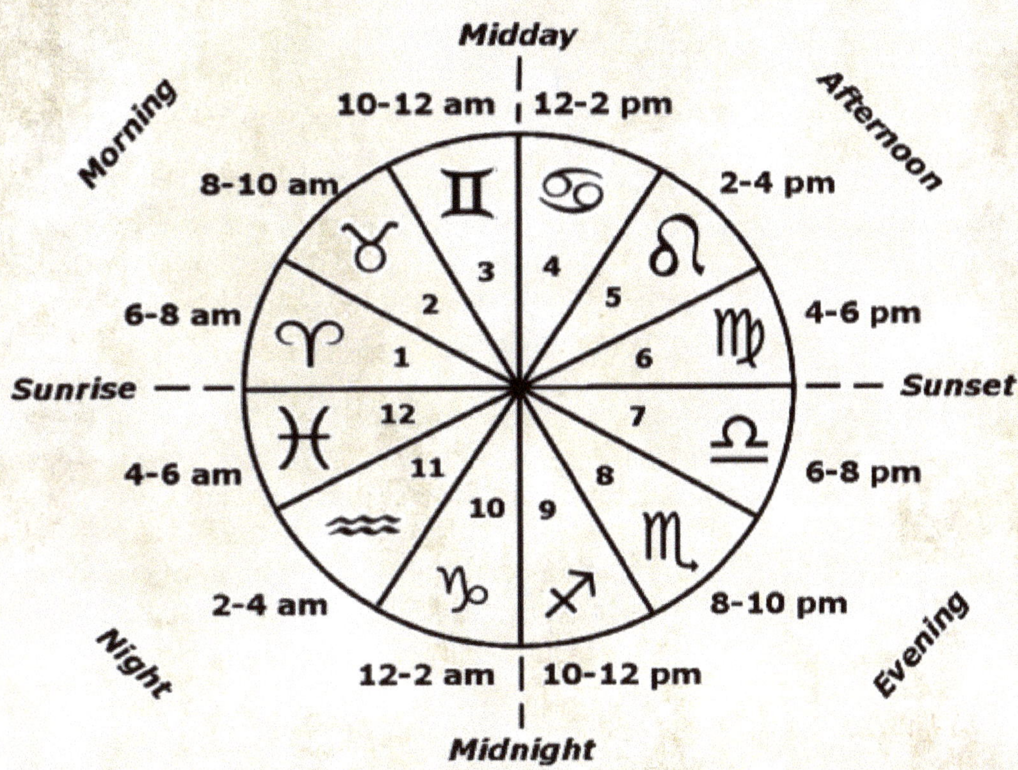

For instance, the sun begins its journey rising in the East every day and at this point it is Aries. *The Light of Egypt, The Science of the Soul and the Stars, volume II, 1999* Thomas H. Burgoyne states: "The condition of our atmosphere and the surrounding objects -vegetation, etc. have a peculiar condition and a magnetism wholly their own when surveyed exactly at sunrise. There is a freshness and peculiar sense of buoyancy not visible at any other time. If this state could be registered by any instrument and compared with any other set periods during the day, it would offer a remarkable contrast. Two hours later there is a very different influence, and at noon there is a wonderful contrast. The same may be said of sunset, and again at midnight; and, lastly, note the difference two hours before dawn. This is the coolest period of the whole twenty-four hours."

"The Zodiac, then, as it applies to the human constitution and the science of astrology, has its foundation in the sun, the centre and source of life to the planet, and the twelve signs are the twelve great spaces of our earth's annual orbit about her solar parent, each one typical of its month, and each month typical of its corresponding action upon our earthly conditions."

The difference between the Tropical and Sidereal Zodiac

A point I wish to highlight is the difference between the tropical zodiac and the sidereal. The tropical zodiac is used in the west and within this book. The sidereal zodiac is primarily used in the east. The tropical zodiac, however, is based upon nature and derived not from the constellations in the Milky Way but from the cycle of the sun's journey around the solar year. The correspondences that we use as western astrologers using the tropical system are a direct result of these observations - the timing is based upon the seasons and observations taken from Nature.

At the point of the Spring Equinox the sun moves into Aries at 0.0 degrees and the 11 other signs follow through in order, each sign accommodating a thirty degree segment on the ecliptic. The sun always enters Cancer at 0.0 degrees at the Summer Solstice, Libra on the Autumn Equinox and Capricorn on the Winter Solstice. Unfortunately, throughout history there has been a lot of confusion and mixed messages given when debating and validating this topic.

The main point raised is the gradual shifting of the constellations and this is true - the sidereal zodiac is moving in reverse motion to the traditional tropical zodiac. Every 2,160 years, each sign retrogrades to the extent of thirty degrees. Our age is shifting from Pisces to that of Aquarius.

Tropical Astrology and Sidereal Astrology have fundamentally different approaches. Tropical Astrology is taken from the observation of nature and cycles, as explained above and not from the constellations called by the same name.

Cardinal - Initiators

Fixed - Stabilisers

Mutable - Adapters

The Cardinal Signs

Spring - Aries - March 21st Spring Equinox, the spark, cardinal fire
Summer - Cancer - June 21st Summer Solstice, freshwater, cardinal water
Autumn - Libra - September 21st Autumn Equinox, gusts of wind, cardinal air
Winter - Capricorn - December 21st Winter Solstice, mountains (formation of rock), cardinal earth

Cardinal Energy – Aries ♈, Cancer ♋, Libra ♎, Capricorn ♑

These four signs start the wheel in motion and represent the beginning of each season, containing the nature of concentrated force. This energy is required to initiate the change of season. Psychologically they are the months of generation and initiation, containing the quality of ambition that can manifest in various guises.

Cardinal signs contain within them active and initiatory force, the drivers of motion.

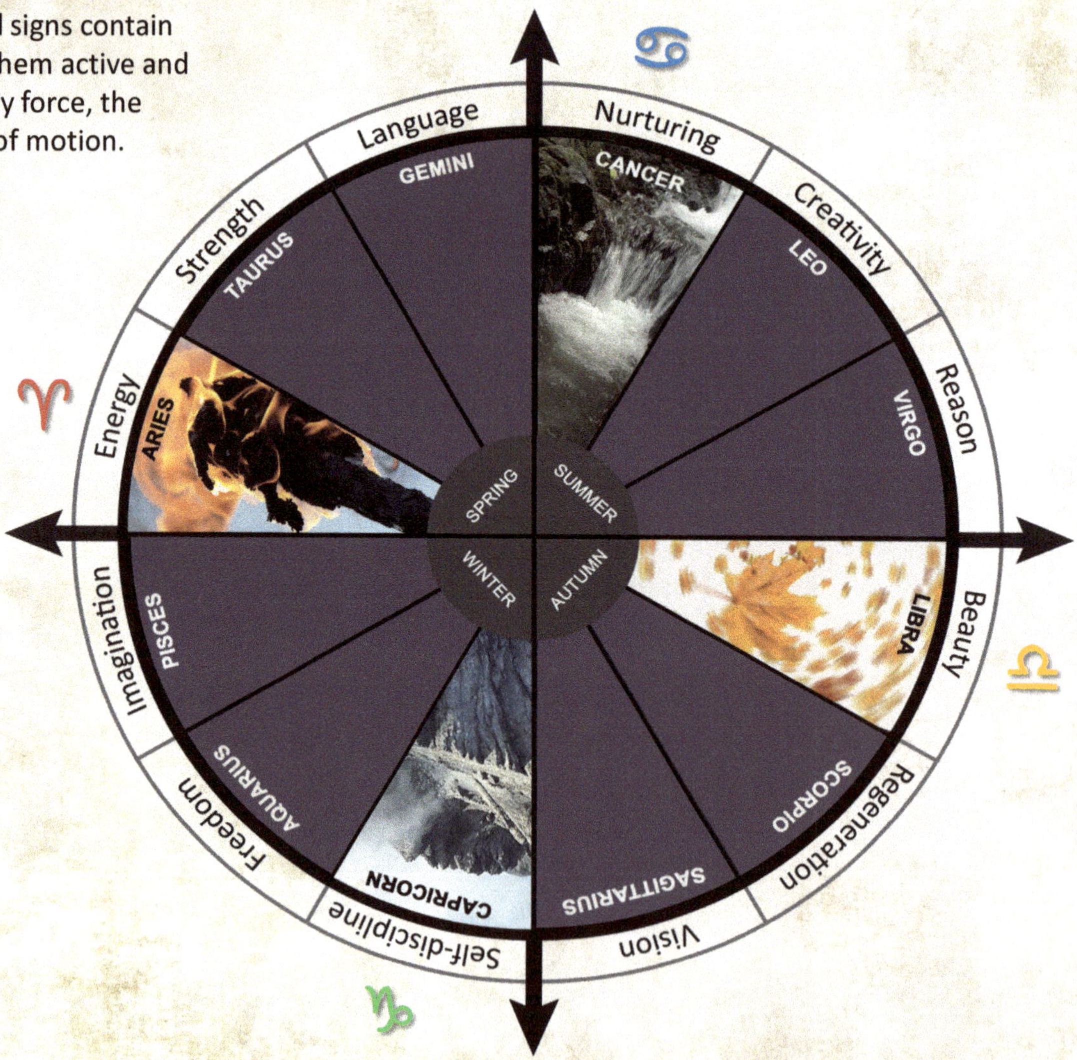

The Fixed Signs

The second astrological month in each season is known as the seasonal peak, when nature has taken hold and becomes established, is depicted by:

Spring - Taurus - Bull, fertile soil, fixed earth
Summer- Leo - Lion, hearth fire, fixed fire
Autumn- Scorpio - Scorpion, eagle, iceberg, fixed water
Winter-Aquarius - Water Bearer, peacock, icy winds, fixed air

Fixed Energy – Taurus ♉, Leo ♌, Scorpio ♏, Aquarius ♒

All these signs contain the quality of strength. Psychologically they are months of operation and stabilisation, sharing the drive of determination and endurance that manifests in various guises. Fixed signs are steadfast, strong, determined and immovable. The second sign in each season is when nature has a firm and determined hold over the element and season.

The Mutable Signs

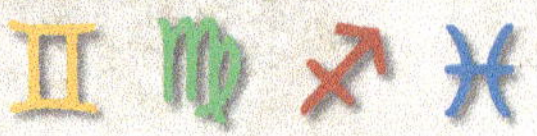

The final month of each season, when nature is adapting and preparing for the inevitable climatic change, is depicted by:

Spring- Gemini - Twins, butterfly, light gentle breezes, mutable air
Summer- Virgo - Virgin, ants, bees, tall tree with deep roots, mutable earth
Autumn-Sagittarius - Centaur, bush fire, mutable fire
Winter- Pisces - Salmon, ocean, mutable water

Mutable Energy – Gemini ♊, Virgo ♍, Sagittarius ♐, Pisces ♓

The mutable signs are the season's finale containing the ability to disperse. They excel at finding resource.   Psychologically they are the months of dissolution, adaptation and communication, sharing the quality of flexibility that manifests in various guises. Mutable signs are adaptable and versatile. The last sign of the season when nature is morphing and transitioning in preparation for the change into a new season.

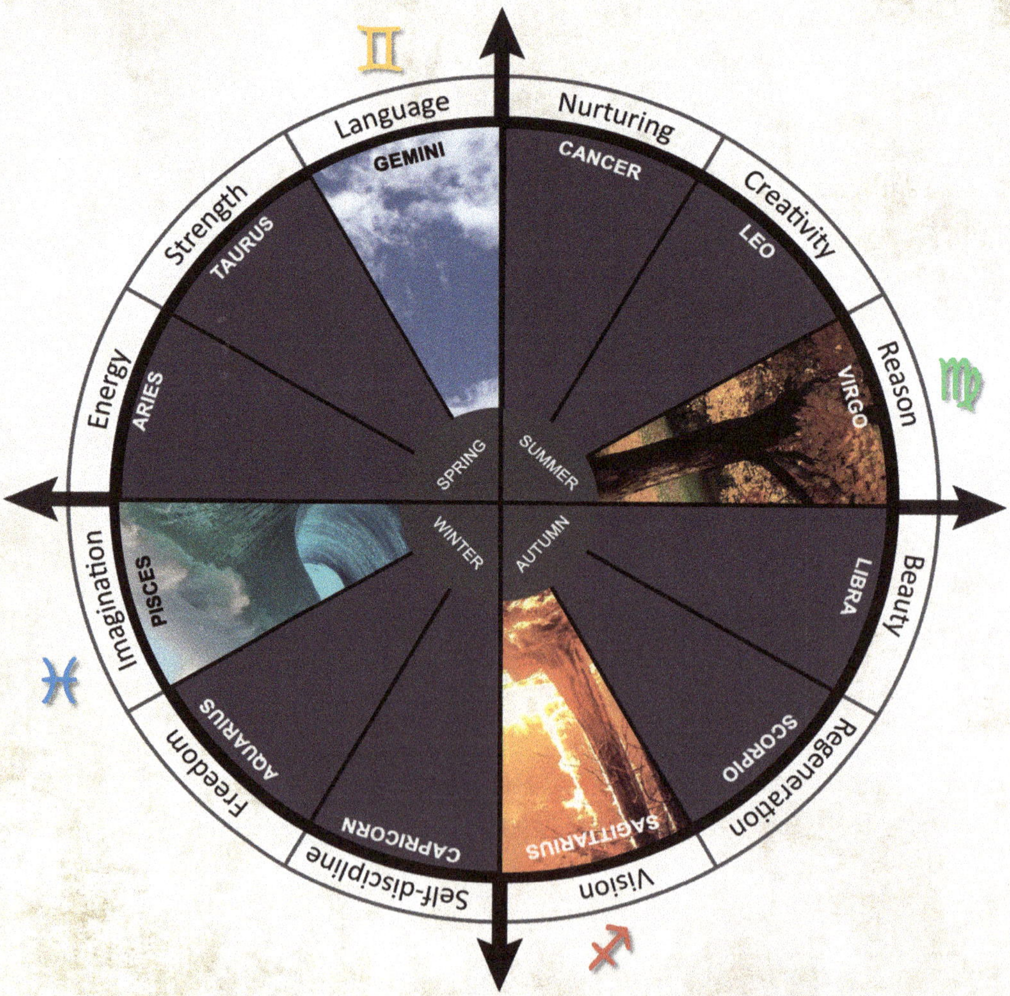

The Four Great Beacons

You may recognise the four points as they are to be found within many disciplines i.e. the Bible, Quran and other scriptures. In the Bible the four is referred to frequently i.e.; the four winds - Daniel 7:2; the four points of the compass - Daniel 11:4; the four spirits of heaven - Zechariah 6:5.   Below shows the four horsemen of revelation. Revelations 4:7 "The first living creature was like a lion, the second was like a bull, the third had the face like a man, the fourth was like a flying eagle."

The horses represent the four Cardinal signs of action - Aries, Cancer, Libra and Capricorn. In the Stoic tradition the four Cardinal points represent the four virtues of Courage, Temperance, Justice and Wisdom. The four horsemen are the Fixed signs of consistency, represented by the Bull, Taurus – Physical; Lion, Leo – Spiritual; Eagle, Scorpio - Emotional; Man, Aquarius - Mental.   These points also make up the 8 spokes of the wheel as celebrated in the Celtic Wheel of the Year.

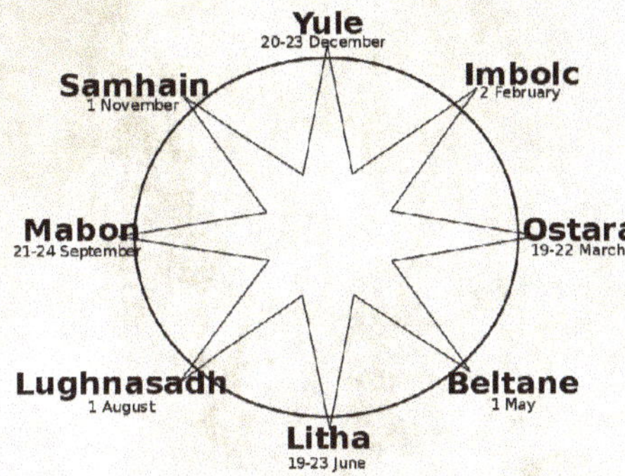

In the Qabalah tradition, the four fixed points are known as the Kerubim, the forces that govern the four elements and are represented as the Eagle - Water; the Bull - Earth; the Lion - Fire and Man - Air. The four Great Beacons of strength. Shown below are pictures of the World tarot card, the spirit of the four elements are seen guarding the four corners of the world.

The Four Horsemen

Universe (Thoth Deck) and World (Rider-Waite) Tarot Cards

The Four Elements

Fire Earth Air Water

We have looked at the forces of Nature - now we are going to look at the elements Fire, Earth, Air and Water. Each solar month has its own element. There is one element for each force of nature i.e. Aries is Cardinal Fire, Leo is Fixed Fire, Sagittarius is Mutable Fire.

On the following pages we will see what happens to these elements when we mix them with natures forces.

Fire represents enthusiasm and is expressive by nature. Aries, Leo, Sagittarius

Earth represents stability and is receptive by nature. Taurus, Virgo, Capricorn

Air represents the Intellect and is expressive by nature. Gemini, Libra, Aquarius

Water represents feelings and is receptive by nature. Cancer, Scorpio, Pisces

Three Stages of Fire

Combining the elements:
Fire needs water to stop it burning out of control, fire needs water to create steam, fire needs earth to burn and bring new life out of the ashes and fire needs air to give it life.

Each element works hand in hand with the other to achieve different states. For instance a rainbow will appear when all the elements are in play.   The elements when mixed with the forces of nature, (Cardinal, Fixed, Mutable), produce a different result. Below we can see how the element fire responds to the different forces.

FIRE
Energy, Enthusiasm, Hope, Love. The Archangel of fire is Michael.
– Element tool is the wand, the wand was originally a torch bringing light. The wand of courage. The vision of hope.

Cardinal Fire - The spark
lighting a match, the beginning.
Force - Aries.

Fixed Fire - The hearth,
the camp fire, contained.
Stabiliser - Leo.

Mutable Fire - The bush fire or wildfire
with no boundaries.
Disperser - Sagittarius.

Three Stages of Earth

Combining the elements:
Earth needs water to be fertile, earth needs air to spread the seed. Earth needs fire to grow - as out of the ashes springs new life. From flowing lava rocks are formed.

The elements when mixed with the forces of nature, (Cardinal, Fixed, Mutable) produce a different result:

EARTH
Stability, Practicality, Law, Service. The Archangel of earth is Uriel.
– Element tool is a disc or tablet, originally a spade to control earth. The disc of strength.
The foundation of understanding.

Cardinal Earth - Mountain rocks, immense pressure released forms mountains.
Force - Capricorn.

Fixed Earth - Ploughed field, fertile and abundant earth.
Stabiliser - Taurus.

Mutable Earth - Tall tree with deep roots, bending to the winds of reason.
Disperser - Virgo.

Three Stages of Air

Combining the elements:
Air brings life to fire, air brings abundance to earth by dispersing the seeds by wind. Air brings movement to water and form by transforming it to ice.

The elements when mixed with the forces of nature, (Cardinal, Fixed, Mutable), produce a different result:

AIR
Thoughts, Intellect, Peace, Brotherhood. The Archangel of air is Raphael.
– Element tool is a sword that cuts through the air. The sword of peace.
The vision of faith.

Cardinal Air - Gusts of wind, air moving in spurts.
Force - Libra.

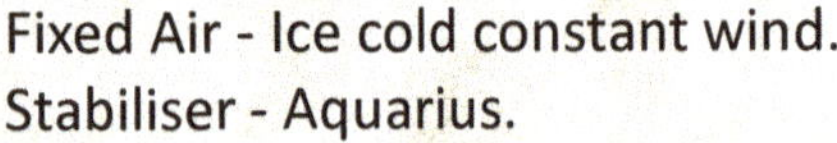

Fixed Air - Ice cold constant wind.
Stabiliser - Aquarius.

Mutable Air - Light breezes, warm Spring air, free movement of air.
Disperser - Gemini.

Three Stages of Water

Combining the elements:
Water needs earth to contain it and water needs fire to heat it and transmute to steam, water needs air to change its motion and structure.

The elements when mixed with the forces of nature, (Cardinal, Fixed, Mutable), produce a different result:

WATER
Feelings, Emotion, Charity, Empathy. The Archangel of water is Gabriel.
– Element tool is a cup or chalice used to contain water. The cup of love.
The vision of Compassion.

Cardinal Water - Babbling brooks and shallow rock pools, fresh water.
Force - Cancer.

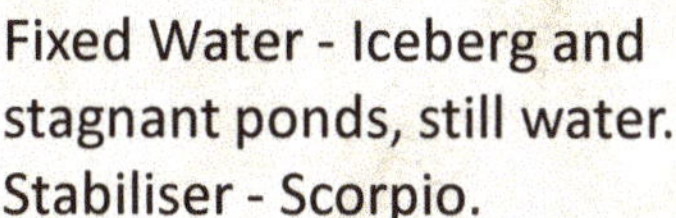

Fixed Water - Iceberg and stagnant ponds, still water.
Stabiliser - Scorpio.

Mutable Water - Sea, waves, water with no containment.
Disperser - Pisces.

Psychological Journey of the Lanterns

Just as the elements grow and mature in stages i.e.; fire begins as the spark, then forms the hearth fire and develops into the stage of the bush fire - there is also the psychological growth of each of the signs.

We have seen that the sun starts its journey at the Spring Equinox with Aries, representing the beginning, birth, energy and psychologically the newborn - a time in life when the primary inner drive is survival. The toddler represents the next phase when a familiar environment is important and he is discovering his senses - this is Taurus. Gemini is the last phase of Spring and this is the infant who has just discovered his voice - a curious and inquisitive time of questioning.

Cancer, the first sign of Summer is represented by the child. When the child starts school, his home is his heart - feelings and emotions come to the fore.   Next in the cycle is the teenager represented by Leo, aware of their creative force, seeking attention and playing at being an adult. Virgo is the student who studies and observes, developing and perfecting his skills with reasoning.

Autumn is represented by Libra, the young adult, when the time has come to find someone with whom to share experiences. Scorpio is a time when superficial relationships are not enough - it is a period to explore deeper feelings and passions. The last phase of Autumn is Sagittarius - the mature adult who seeks to explore and discover horizons within himself and, the world around him.

Winter is the last phase and begins with the sign Capricorn and middle age. A time when we use the experience of our life to materially secure our position and through discipline, prepare for the future. Mid winter is Aquarius, the age of retirement when there is time to do the things we have always wanted to do - it brings with it freedom. We end this psychological journey with Pisces - late winter, old age when the imagination takes flight, the veil is beginning to thin between the astral worlds and earth.

Psychological Cycle

Season	Lantern	Sign	Phase	Root
Spring	Energy	Aries	Newborn	I Am
Mid Spring	Strength	Taurus	Toddler	I Have
Late Spring	Language	Gemini	Infant	I Think
Summer	Nurturing	Cancer	Child	I Feel
Mid Summer	Creativity	Leo	Teenager	I Will
Late Summer	Reason	Virgo	Student	I Observe
Autumn	Beauty	Libra	Young Adult	I Relate
Mid Autumn	Regeneration	Scorpio	Lover	I Desire
Late Autumn	Vision	Sagittarius	Adult	I Discover
Winter	Self-Discipline	Capricorn	Middle Age	I Use
Mid Winter	Freedom	Aquarius	Retirement	I Know
Late Winter	Imagination	Pisces	Old Age	I Believe

Planetary Rulers

There is a fountain of knowledge to be discovered within the 12 Lanterns. The table below shows the correspondences for the lanterns aligned with their planetary rulers. Each planet represents an urge or drive within us.

Lantern	Sign	Planet	Urge
Energy	Aries	Mars	Survive
Strength	Taurus	Venus	Manifest
Language	Gemini	Mercury	Communicate
Nurturing	Cancer	Moon	Respond
Creativity	Leo	Sun	Live
Reason	Virgo	Mercury	Serve
Beauty	Libra	Venus	Love
Regeneration	Scorpio	Pluto	Transform
Vision	Sagittarius	Jupiter	Grow
Self-discipline	Capricorn	Saturn	Control
Freedom	Aquarius	Uranus	Change
Imagination	Pisces	Neptune	Dream

The exercises in this booklet ask you to write down the answers to certain questions for reflection later. Through having your birth chart compiled you will be able to gain further insight into your responses and the different areas of your life. Astrology shows you what you already know. It gives an anchor, a structure, a foundation to understanding the self. We are a synthesised mix of the signs and have a different way of expressing our urges through different signs depending upon the date, time and place of birth.

1. The planets are the individual urge to express their essential nature.
2. The zodiac signs are the kind of expression and attitude that takes.
3. The houses are the areas of life where the planets express themselves.
4. The aspects show if the individual finds ease or difficulty in expression.

Astrology and the Tree of Life

You will see diagrams on each lantern relating to the Tree of Life. It is a map that allows us to build upon our inner awareness and learn about our personality; understand our soul and experience our spirit. On each lantern section the corresponding sphere will be highlighted. Each sign and lantern is ruled by a planet. Each planet is representative of the energy and force of the spheres *(sephiroh)* in which they reside on the Tree of Life. Understanding the energy behind the symbolism shows us the force/drive it represents and allows us to recognise it in everyday life. We can see from the diagram below that the sun is still in the centre, as it is also at the centre of our solar system, representing the heart of ourselves. The pathways that link the spheres together correspond with the tarot cards (*In diagram; Thoth Deck*), the Hebrew letters, zodiac signs and elements.

TWO
Lighting the Lanterns Within

Approaching the Lantern Pathworkings

We are ready to begin our magical journey of the astrological Shining Lanterns - a journey that starts at the point of Aries at the Spring Equinox and continues its pathway around the solar year to finish at Pisces, otherwise known as the 'Wheel of the Year.' Along the way we will discover that the light of the sun is different depending upon the thirty degree segment of the path upon which you are standing. The sun's rays are split into twelve, shining their hue through each lantern, highlighting the underlying essence of each sign, which has it roots in the Tree of Life.

The lanterns unfold in four stages as below; our example is based upon the Lantern of Beauty.
1. Study the zodiac sign preparation with its correspondences.
2. Contemplate the Motivational Reminder for the solar time of year.
3. Learn about the many forces that sit within the lantern.
4. Complete the exercises to see how each Lantern is working within your life.

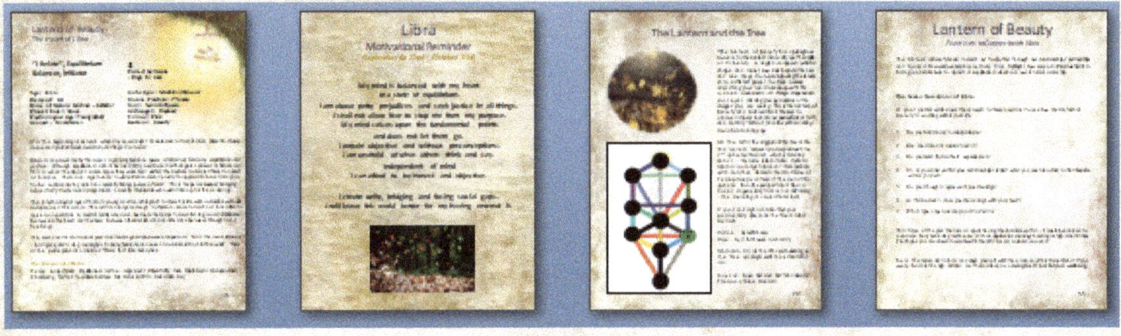

| Step 1 | Step 2 | Step 3 | Step 4 |

As each month has its function and purpose in nature - from the buds appearing in spring to the starkness and decay of winter - so do we. The preparation step reveals each time of the year has a psychological age, animal, season, element and mindset. *(Dates vary slightly from year to year so if looking up your sun sign please see an ephemeris for the actual dates for the year you were born. The date when the sun moves into a sign can vary from 20th- 23rd).*

Use the Motivational Reminder on step two to refocus your mind and align your motivation. Step three reveals the essence of the Lantern, contemplate this to light up that part of yourself. On step four there are seven questions for each lantern - it is useful to write down your answers to the questions in a journal or notebook so that you will be able to reflect upon insights revealed and how that lantern is operating within your life as you walk the path. *See page three in the Introduction Section for more information on lighting the lantern within.*

Archetypal correspondences are listed under each sign as you travel with the sun through the zodiac for that time of year. As stated previously we are made up of not just one lantern but have within us the framework of all 12 and this template can be used to assist us throughout our whole life. Becoming aware of the time of year and aligning with nature's correspondences - through direct correlation with the world around you, allows you to discover your potential and how these influences work within you.

The Spring Lanterns
Aries, Taurus, Gemini

Lantern of Energy
Aries, Cardinal Fire

March 21st – April 20th

Lantern of Strength
Taurus, Fixed Earth

April 21st – May 20th

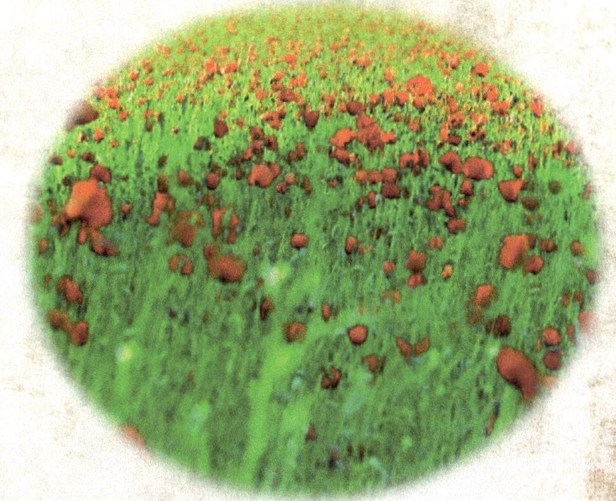

Lantern of Language
Gemini, Mutable Air

May 21st – June 20th

Lantern of Energy
The Heart of Aries

"I Am," The Spark
Warrior, Initiator

♂
Ruled by Mars
- Urge to survive

Sign: **Aries**
Element: **Fire**
Force of Nature: **Cardinal - Initiator**
Planet Ruler: **Mars**
Psychological Age: **Newborn**
Animal: **Ram**

Archetype: **Warrior**
House Position: **1ˢᵗ house**
Tool: **Wand of courage**
Time of Year: **Spring Equinox, Ostara**
Colour: **Red**
Lantern: **Energy**

Welcome to Aries and the first solar month of Spring. It brings with it initiatory, dynamic, fresh energy as nature bursts into colour. Aries is the element of cardinal fire. It is new, raw, the beginning of a cycle when all that was hidden now sparks and emerges into the light. The days are equal to the nights and the sun becomes warmer, colour begins to form all around us and animals instinctively sense the awakening - it is time to mate to produce new life.

The animal associated with Aries is the Ram. In order to ensure that the alpha male is the strongest in the pack, he will instinctively and energetically charge towards the challenger with his head down, unaware of any other dangers that may be lurking in his fight for supremacy.

We can liken this behaviour to that of the psychological age of a newborn - helpless, innocent, naive and fearless. Heightened survival instinct, noisy and demanding, if his basic needs are not met.

The mindset of Aries is one of raw energy bursting to the surface in fits and starts, requiring action. To be engaged in the fires of life, to be where the action is, the one who starts the fire. Ambitious, impatient, a force of willpower, for this is the instinctive Warrior who initiates motion and takes up the sword to fight injustices.

The Keywords of Aries
Newborn, Fire, Beginning, Initiator, Survival, Impulsive, Instincts, Daring, Fearless, Warrior, Vindicator, Naive, Innocent, Impatient, Enthusiastic, Pioneering, Entrepreneur, Willpower, Action, Selfish, Angry.

Aries
Motivational Reminder
(Spring Solstice ♈ March 21st - April 20th)

I am that I am, I am the spark that creates life,
I am unconquerably fearless.
I have courage and energy to meet all life's challenges.
Success is coming, if not immediately, then I can wait.
I am the initiator that does not doubt,
as I weigh up all things.

I will see my plans through with enthusiasm,
positivity, sincerity and enterprise.
I meet opposition and competitors without bitterness.
I remain open and forthright to all who cross my path.
Nothing can shake my core; I am strong and resolute.

Through my flash of creativity,
I improve on the ways of yesterday.

The Lantern and the Tree

The Lantern of Energy is a single flickering golden flame - the beginning, birth and the spark of creation. Look deeper into the flame and the image of a warrior is revealed, full of energy, heightened survival instinct and ready for action. It holds within it the key to our own energy and will.

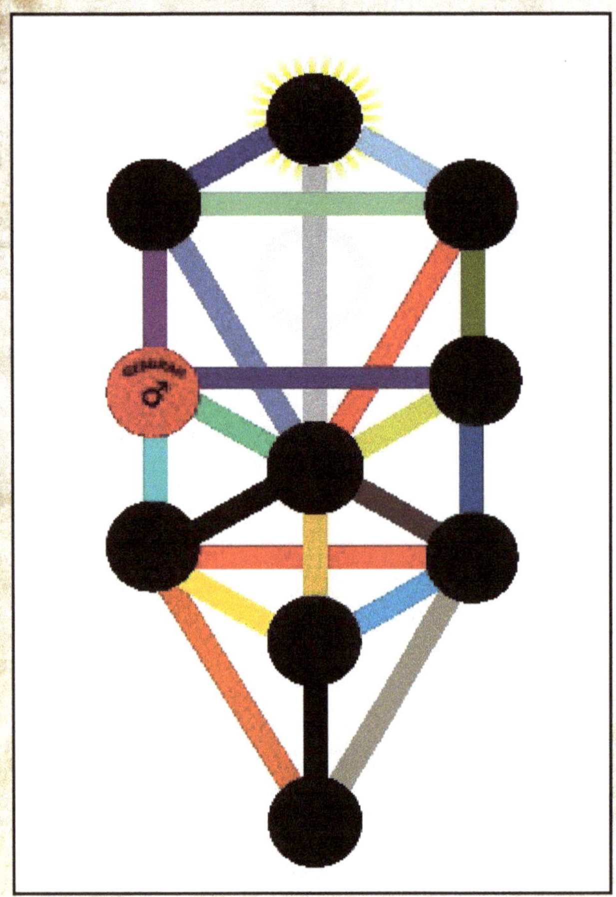

On the left is the diagram of The Tree of Life. The Lantern of Energy corresponds with the 5th sphere of Geburah which is ruled by the planet Mars - the same ruler of Aries. Mars is a planet of action and is our urge to survive.

Here sits the philosophy of the Cosmic Law of Karma, the word karma means action and this law is often referred to as the Law of Cause and Effect. This sphere contains the roots of willpower and conscience within it.

If your sun sign is in Aries then your personality sphere on the Tree of Life is Geburah.

Virtue: **Energy and courage**
Vice: **Cruelty and destruction**

Aries sits on the 15th pathworking on the Tree and aligns with the Emperor tarot card.

Incense: **Tobacco, Basil, Copal, Cinnamon**
Precious Stone: **Ruby, Garnet**

Exercises for Connection

This is the time of year for sowing seeds, for taking action and initiating projects, to start the build. What projects are waiting for you to take action on? It is a good idea to write these down, make a list, so that you can cross them off later.

Become aware of your physical body and its exercise needs. As the first month of Spring is a time of high raw energy, it is important to give this a positive outlet, as in some people, this energy can turn to impatience, frustration and anger. Look to physical activities including 'spring cleaning.' Clear out the clutter to make way for new growth.

This is the part of you that can at times feel vulnerable - like a newborn. A newborn's primary instinct is the urge to survive.

The Seven Questions of Aries

In your journal, write down the answers to these questions to see how the Lantern of Energy is working within your life.

1. How do you feel when you hold a baby?

2. This Lantern of energy contains the force to initiate enthusiasm - how easy is it for you to do this?

3. The planet Mars aligns with this lantern. It represents our driving force within. Where is your energetic driving force - what makes you move?

4. In what area of life can you really be yourself?

5. In which areas of your life do you feel fearless towards?

6. What area of your life do you jump in feet first?

7. Become aware of your survival instincts and recognise how they work for you.

Please read the reminder to focus and align yourself with the essence of the time of year. If you were born in the sign of Aries, use the reminder as a realignment tool for your wellbeing.

Look at where Aries sits in your birth chart and the area of life it governs - where do you dive right in? Look to Mars to see what survival means to you.

One tree can start a forest,
One bird can herald spring,
One smile can begin a friendship,
One hand can lift a soul,
One star can guide a ship at sea,
One word can frame the goal,
One sunbeam can light a room,
One candle can wipe out darkness,
One laugh can conquer gloom,
One hope can raise our spirits,
One touch can show you care,
One voice can wake up everybody,
One life can make the difference.
Be that one.
-Author Unknown

Lantern of Strength
The Heart of Taurus

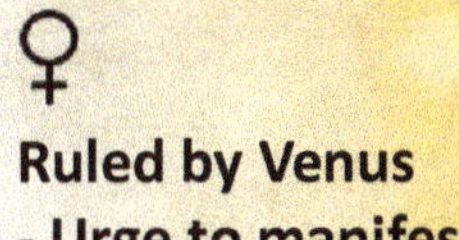

**"I Have," Sustainer
Builder, Stabiliser**

♀

**Ruled by Venus
- Urge to manifest**

Sign: **Taurus**
Element: **Earth**
Force of Nature: **Fixed - Sustainer**
Planet Ruler: **Venus**
Psychological Age: **Toddler**
Animal: **Bull**

Archetype: **Builder**
House Position: **2nd house**
Tool: **Disc of strength**
Time of the Year: **Beltane, 15° Taurus**
Colour: **Green**
Lantern: **Strength**

Taurus is the second month of spring when the land becomes fertile and ripe for planting. This is the element of fixed earth indicating consistency, predictability and warm abundance. Fragrant smells fill the air, stimulating our senses, and bright colours are all around.

The bull is the animal associated with Taurus - the strong, patient, contented browsing animal. As long as he is in familiar territory (as alien things disturb him), he will happily chew on the cud and frolic in his own paddock. Nothing quite touches a person born at this time of year; it appears as though he is immune and protected from the everyday knocks of the other months. If you leave him undisturbed he is peaceful and will happily protect his territory and the things he values. If he meets something he does not understand, then he will create a loud dramatic scene like a 'bull in a china shop' until he gets some clarity.

The psychological age is that of the toddler who uses his senses to discover his surroundings - he thinks that everything he touches is his and he has to be taught that sharing is rewarding; he also likes to be comfortable. The energy of Taurus brings determination, stamina and endurance - qualities needed for the stabilisation and operation of life.

The mindset of this time of year is the urge to manifest and unfold a sense of true meaning and value in life. This is the sustainer.

The keywords of Taurus
Determined, Persistent, Stable, Stamina, Comfort, Patient, Sensual, Enduring, Strong, Steadfast, Sustenance, Conventional, Practical, Plodder, Morals, Senses, Values, Dogmatic, Stubborn.

Taurus
Motivational Reminder
(April ♉ 21st - May 20th)

My strength comes from my heart,
I am a constant force;
learning from everybody and every incident of my life.
Nothing upsets my calmness of mind.
I think out every step, every word,
with painstaking care and deliberation.
My head works with reasoning and I act wisely.
I reserve judgement - I do not run with the crowd.
My foundations are solid and my courage unshakeable.
I treat the whole world courteously and with conscience.
I am steadfast, reliable and loyal.
All those who know me feel that I am intensely fair.

I welcome challenges; they make me more
determined than ever.

The Lantern and the Tree

The **Lantern of Strength** is shining a light green consistent glow, lighting up the next segment. Look deeper into the flame and you see a fertile field, resplendent with red poppies - a contented bull full of strength and solidity, stares back at you. This bull is at home with familiar things; he likes to be comfortable within his environment as consistency sustains his nature. This is the Lantern of Strength and holds the key to our own core and internal strength.

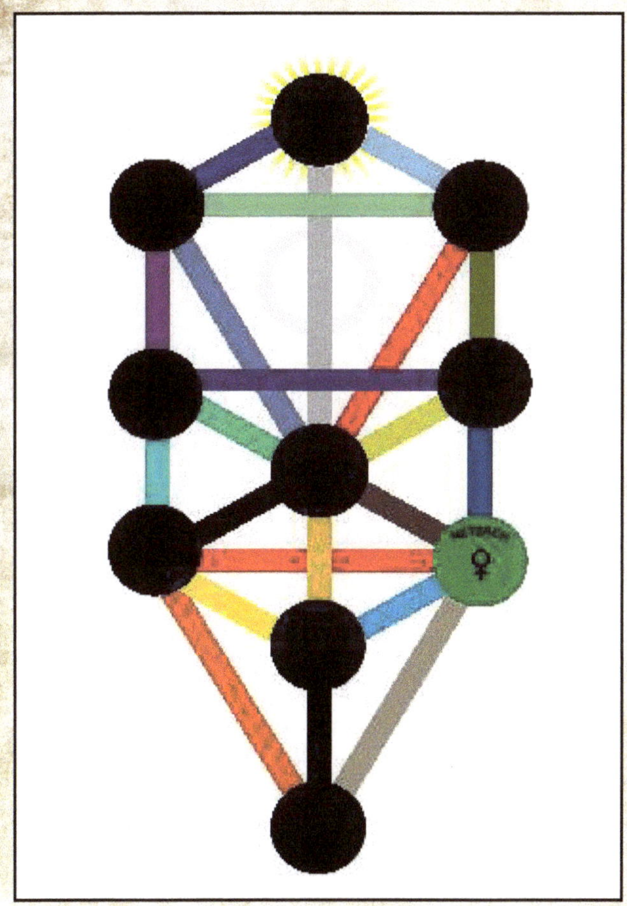

The Lantern of Strength corresponds with the 7th sphere of Netzach which is ruled by the planet Venus - the same ruler of Taurus. Venus is a planet of feeling and when aligning with Taurus is our urge to love and manifest.

Here sits the Cosmic Law of Perception. This sphere contains the power of the spirit or forces that exist within Nature, the feelings of desire and passion that inspire and stimulate the imagination.

If your sun sign is in Taurus then your personality sphere on the Tree of Life is Netzach.

Virtue: **Unselfishness**
Vice: **Lust for Power**

Taurus sits on the 16th pathworking on the Tree and aligns with the Hierophant tarot card.

Incense: **Rose, Sandalwood, Benzoin**
Precious Stone: **Emerald, Malachite**

Exercises for Connection

This is the time to use your determination to build upon or sustain a project that has been started. To see things through, to provide nourishment, when many give up and walk away.

The lantern of Strength shows us the persistency within us to get what we really want but the first step is to know what you really want. Our wants are very different from our needs - our needs are born from our survival instincts, our wants are born from our desires.

The Seven Questions of Taurus

In your journal, write down the answers to these questions to see how the Lantern of Strength is working within your life.

1. Make a list of 5 things that you really want ...

2. Ask yourself how determined you are!

3. How much stamina do you have to stay the course?

4. What tools do you have that will help make what you want happen?

5. When do you feel out of your comfort zone?

6. What things disturb you?

7. How important are material gains to you?

We are spiritual beings operating through our physical body. Connect with your 5 senses: taste, touch, sight, smell and sound to increase your awareness of your self and your environment. You can do this by spending time outdoors in a natural environment like the countryside.

Read the reminder to focus and align yourself with the essence of this time of year.   If you were born in the sign of Taurus, use the reminder as a realignment tool for your wellbeing.

Look at where Taurus sits in your birth chart and the area of life it governs - how much stamina do you have? Look to Venus to understand your drive to manifest.

'A good head and a good heart

are always a formidable

combination.'

Nelson Mandela

Lantern of Language
The Heart of Gemini

"I Think," Communication
Messenger, Resourcer

☿

Ruled by Mercury
- Urge to communicate

Sign: **Gemini**
Element: **Air**
Force of Nature: **Mutable - Resourcer**
Planet Ruler: **Mercury**
Psychological Age: **Infant**
Animal: **Butterfly/Twins**

Archetype: **Messenger**
House Position: **3rd house**
Tool: **Sword of peace**
Time of Year: **Spring finale**
Colour: **Yellow**
Lantern: **Language**

Welcome to the last solar month of spring when nature is morphing and adapting to welcome a new season. This is the element of mutable air. Light warm breezes fill the air and butterflies flit from flower to flower, dancing and flirting from scent to scent.

The human twins are associated with Gemini which indicates duality, the light and the dark sides of our nature and the ability to see things in black and white. This is the adaptable mind that flits backwards and forwards, offering two opposing opinions on the same subject, on the same day. There is an urge to communicate, to gossip, to be frivolous, witty and spread the word.

This is the essence of language, the art of socialising, uniting communities. Curiosity is at its height and there is a desire to know something about everything and pass that knowledge on. The logical mind is active, alive, versatile and understands the abstract.

The psychological age of Gemini is that of an infant who has just found his voice and is eagerly asking questions - what, why, how, where and when.

The mindset of this time of year is that of messengers such as Hermes, Thoth, Mercury, Moses and St Paul. To share knowledge with clarity so that all may understand the reality and truth of what is being conveyed.

The Keywords of Gemini:
Communication, Messenger, Resourceful, Curious, Inquisitive, Adaptable, Changeable, Logical, Witty, Intelligent, Mischievous, Talkative, Restless, Superficial, Cerebral, Clever, Flirty, Sarcastic, Irritable.

Gemini
Motivational Reminder
(May Ⅱ 21st - June 20th)

My mind is alert, astute and functioning well.
Though I see and hear with clarity, I think kindly.
When I see clearly, I know instinctively, the right course.
I will not be distracted by frivolity once I begin a task.
In all my work I display conscientiousness
and discrimination.
With skilful accuracy I choose to set my sights high.
In every way I keep in mind the essentials
and master details first.

Nerves will not get the better of me - they exist as servants,
they do not control me; realising this I become strong .

I have faith in myself and my abilities.

The Lantern and the Tree

The Lantern of Language welcomes us. It is a bright yellow light dancing and flitting around. Looking deeper into the lantern we see tiny sylphs - the elemental beings of air - hovering and playing, frolicking in the soft warm breeze. Butterflies flit from one brightly coloured flower to another.   This is the Lantern of Language and holds the key to our attitude and communication.

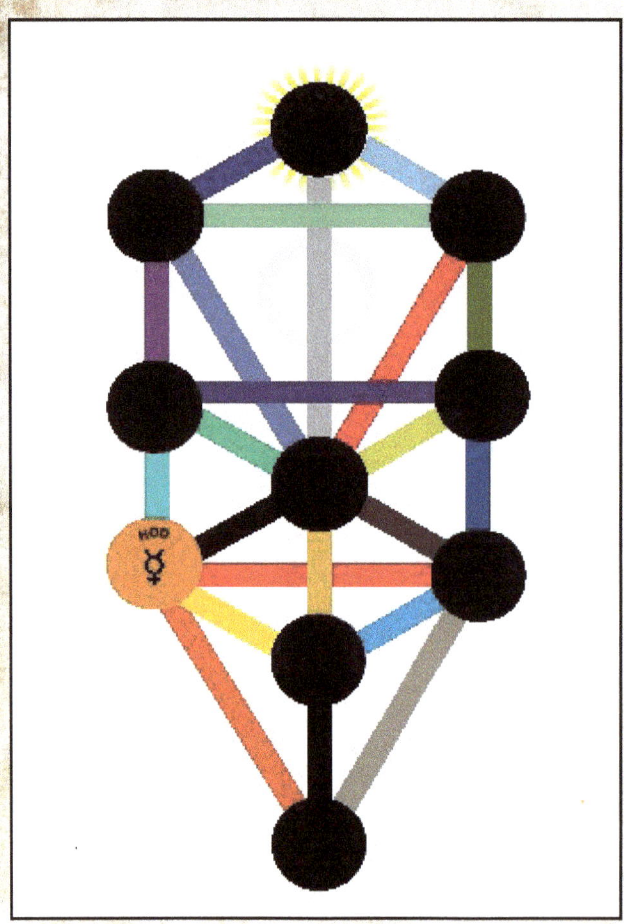

The Lantern of Language corresponds with the 8th sphere of Hod which is ruled by the planet mercury - the same ruler of Gemini. Mercury is a planet of the mind and is our urge to communicate.

Here sits the Cosmic Law of Images. This sphere contains the power to build truthful, clear images, creating the form in the mind before expression.

If your sun sign is in Gemini then your personality sphere on the Tree of Life is Hod.

Virtue: **Truthfulness**
Vice: **Falsehood, dishonesty**

Gemini sits on the 17th pathworking on the Tree and aligns with the Lovers tarot card.

Incense: **Storax, Rosemary, Wisteria**
Precious Stone: **Opal, Citrine, Amber**

Exercises for Connection

The energy of the Lantern of Language is beneficial in order to trigger learning, assisting us in absorbing facts and information, communicating with others and building clear images and thought forms - via writing, speaking or even through body language. There is an expression of communication that is seeking to be heard.   The Lantern of Language also asks us to look at our attitude and the effect that it has on others.

The Seven Questions of Gemini

In your journal, write down the answers to these questions to see how the Lantern of Language is working within your life.

1. What type of attitude do you have?

2. How does your attitude affect others?

3. What thoughts keep going round in your mind?

4. Do you feel anxious at any point - and if so, what is the trigger for this?

5. Do you think things through logically?

6. Are you driven by facts or by opinions?

7. How easy is it to visualise and build clear images in your mind? Practice building images within your mind as this can be a useful exercise to give clarity to a project or something that you wish to achieve.

Undertake a detailed visualisation exercise to see how easy it is for you to recall those images afterwards - this exercise can increase memory, concentration and focus.

Gemini rules the nervous system so at this time, boost your magnesium and B vitamin intake.

Read the reminder to focus and align yourself with the essence of the time of year.   If you were born in the sign of Gemini, use the reminder as a realignment tool for your wellbeing.

Look at where Gemini sits in your birth chart and the area of life it governs – how social are you? Look to Mercury to determine your drive to communicate.

The Flow of the Mind
Conscious Empowerment

A diagram of the flow of the mind of consciousness with three sections: the higher mind, the subconscious mind and the conscious mind.

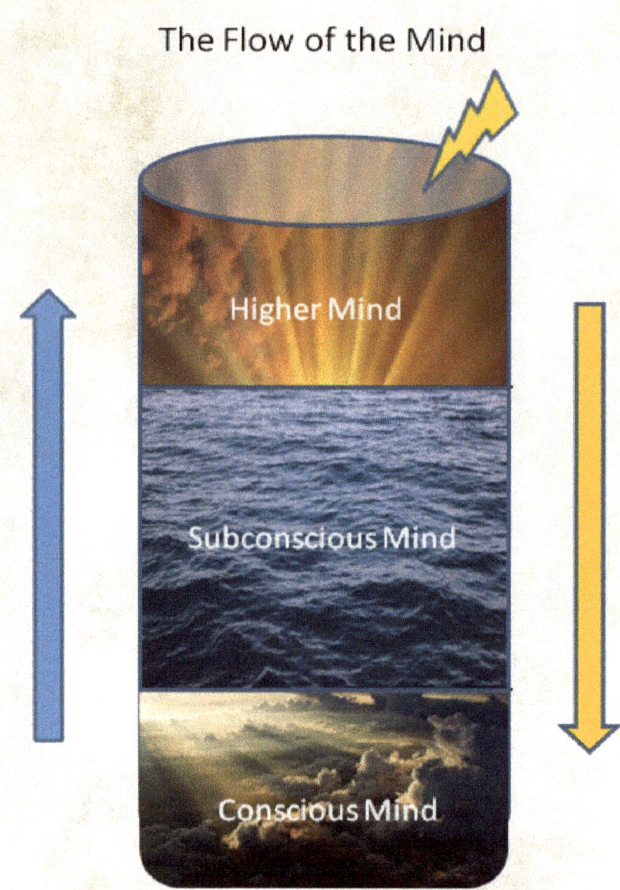

It is important to feed our conscious mind with daily input. The conscious mind is constantly hungry.

Our subconscious mind is our storehouse, responding to symbols and can either be our treasure trove or our dustbin, depending upon how we utilise and maintain it.

The higher mind is the overseer and place of intuition.

Spring Season
Famous persons born in Aries, Taurus, Gemini

Cardinal Fire, Aries
Leonardo Di Vinci, Al Pacino, Sir Alec Guinness, Charlotte Bronte, Hans Christian Anderson, Robert Downey Jr, Francis Ford Coppola, Kofi Annan, Adolf Hitler, Hugh Hefner, Omar Sharif, Steven Seagal, Thomas Jefferson, Sarah Michelle Geller, Sean Bean, Maisie Williams.

Fixed Earth, Taurus
Bing Crosby, Fred Astaire, Engelbert Humperdinck, Audrey Hepburn, Karl Marx, Sigmund Freud, Michael Palin, Orson Welles, Rudolph Valentino, Tony Blair, George Clooney, Tchaikovsky, Bono, Florence Nightingale, George Lucas, Cate Blanchett, Pierce Brosnan, Alexander Ludwig.

Mutable Air, Gemini
Marilyn Monroe, Morgan Freeman, Alanis Morisette, Angelina Jolie, Dalai Lama, Liam Neeson, Tom Jones, Joan Rivers, Johnny Depp, Natalie Portman, Michael J Fox, David Rockefeller, Donald Trump, Boris Johnson, Paul McCartney, John Goodman, Peter Dinklage.

The Summer Lanterns
Cancer, Leo, Virgo

Lantern of Nurturing
Cancer, Cardinal Water

June 21st –July 20th

Lantern of Creativity
Leo, Fixed Fire

July 21st – August 20th

Lantern of Reason
Virgo, Mutable Earth

August 21st – September 21st

Lantern of Nurturing
The Heart of Cancer

"I Feel," Carer
Protector, Initiator

☽
Ruled by the Moon
- Urge to respond

Sign: **Cancer**
Element: **Water**
Force of Nature: **Cardinal - Initiator**
Planet Ruler: **Moon**
Psychological Age: **Child**
Animal: **Crab/Elephant**

Archetype: **Carer**
House Position: **4th house**
Tool: **Cup of love**
Time of Year: **Summer Solstice, Litha**
Colour: **Silver/Pearl**
Lantern: **Nurturing**

Cancer represents the first stage of summer when the sun reaches the zenith - it is at its height. The plants, having budded early in the Spring, are now fully formed. This is the element of cardinal water. Shallow salty rock pools rise in temperature, becoming an oasis for sea life - crabs hide under the rocks and crevices. Freshwater rivers flow towards the sea, babbling brooks become places for bathing. The beginning of a new season brings initiative with tenacious resilience.

The crab is associated with Cancer, having a hard shell to protect it from predators and disguising its soft underbelly of emotional empathy. The crab carries his home and hoards his memories of the ages upon his back. Home, family and his roots are never far from his thoughts.

The psychological age of Cancer is the child who is starting school and home provides the emotional foundation, so they can be confident, within a new environment. This is the essence of nurturing, feeling, protecting and caring.

The mindset of this time of year is just like the behaviour of the crab - one that never takes its eye off the destination even if it appears to be walking sideways. The highly capable yet unassuming Cancer will come from nowhere and take the prize at the last minute to the amazement of those around him. There is a quiet ambition that simmers within.

The Keywords of Cancer:
Protective, Caring, Nurturing, Nourishing, Empathic, Receptive, Manipulative, Ambitious, Defensive, Self-Reliant, Tough, Intuitive, Homely, Funny, Traditional, Nostalgic, Procrastinate, Shy.

Cancer
Motivational Reminder
(June ♋ 21st - July 20th)

I set my imagination to work to create success.
I form a clear vision of the success I want.
Every thought I have is under my instruction,
I refuse to be swayed by my own emotions.
My heart works to the dictation of this reasoning
and I am strong.
Through nurturing, I protect and care.
I radiate goodwill and kindness wherever I go.
I am prepared so there is no fear of failure.
Unhelpful thoughts cannot move me from my purpose.

I set the wheels in motion and lead towards victory
with focus and tenacity.

The Lantern and the Tree

The Lantern of Nurturing has a silvery shimmering glow shining onto the path. As you gaze into the lantern you see a bright summer's day with a cascade of fresh, cleansing, freshwater as it descends from the mountains in the north. These are waters of life, reflection and memory, nurturing and nourishing the earth so that we may have a foundation of growth. This is the Lantern of Nurturing and holds the key to our root foundations.

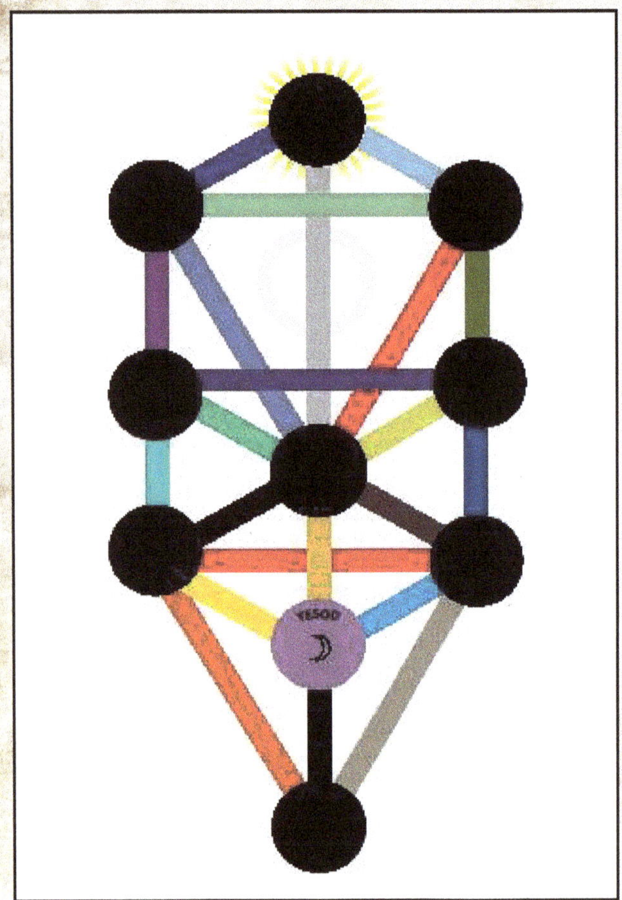

The Lantern of Nurturing corresponds with the 9th sphere of Yesod, which is ruled by the moon - the same ruler of Cancer. The moon represents the tides of our emotions and is our urge to respond.

Here sits the Cosmic Law of Reflection. This sphere contains the 'Hall of Mirrors' providing the tools to recall memories and forgotten information.

If your sun sign is in Cancer then your personality sphere on the Tree of Life is Yesod.

Virtue: **Independence**
Vice: **Idleness**

Cancer sits on the 18th pathworking on the Tree and aligns with the Chariot tarot card.

Incense: **Jasmine, Ginseng, Lavender**
Precious Stone: **Quartz, Pearl, Amethyst**

Exercises for Connection

The energy of this time of year is all about reconnecting with family connections, close friends or those whom you call family. Root foundations and memories are close to the surface and feelings of nostalgia linger.

Connect with the energy of the Lantern of Nurturing by looking around you to see who and what would benefit from some nurturing. Touch base with family members and close friends. Add some homely touches to your living accommodation.

The Seven Questions of Cancer

In your journal, write down the answers to these questions to see how the Lantern of Nurturing is working within your life.

1. What around you needs nurturing to bring it into full bloom?

2. How easy is it for you to nurture something?

3. How important is emotional security to you?

4. Ask yourself what your emotional foundations are like...

5. Do any childhood memories spring to mind?

6. What was/is your relationship like with your mother?

7. Are you a moody person?

The Lantern of Nurturing contains the mirror of reflection and the seeds to recall memories and forgotten information. Symbols act as a trigger, stimulating the subconscious mind. Learning ancient symbols and their meaning can allow easier access and recall when accessing the subconscious mind.

Read the reminder to focus and align yourself with the essence of this time of year.   If you were born in the sign of Cancer, use the reminder as a realignment tool for your wellbeing.

Look at where Cancer sits in your birth chart and the area of life it governs - where do you express your nurturing side? Look to the Moon to identify how you respond.

Lantern of Creativity
The Heart of Leo

"I Will," Creative Force
Leader, Stabiliser

☉

Ruled by the Sun
- Urge to live

Sign: **Leo**
Element: **Fire**
Force of Nature: **Fixed - Stabiliser**
Planet Ruler: **Sun**
Psychological Age: **Teenager**
Animal: **Lion**

Archetype: **Leader**
House Position: **5th house**
Tool: **Wand of courage**
Time of Year: **Lammas (Lughnasadh), 15° Leo**
Colour: **Orange/Gold**
Lantern: **Creativity**

Summer has established a consistent momentum and radiates the heat of the sun. This is the element of fixed fire. People flock to the beaches to bask in the sun and soak up the heat. Just as people flock around a hearth fire in winter, the sun's warm glow is comforting and inviting.

The animal associated with Leo is the mighty lion, who is the king of the beasts - proud, courageous, benevolent and magnanimous, exuding beauty and strength. The leader of noble birth, shining his light upon the world. A big heart, with grand gestures of affection, he expects loyalty and honesty in return. He waits for his audience to linger before him, warming themselves on the steady flame in his heart.

The psychological age is that of the teenager when the pull towards the adult world is beckoning yet they still swing back to the child. A rebellious streak rises to the fore while this transition takes place. They are a child at heart but like to act out the role of authority. Independence is calling and at this age they experiment with their own creative expression and start to feel the impact of their power.

The mindset of this time of year is one of confidence, of feeling and owning one's personal power. It is the essence of the creative force and of self realisation. Courage and boldness can burn away mental restrictions and fire the creative minds of others. There is a desire to achieve control over the personality and an urge toward self-mastery.

The Keywords of Leo:
Pride, Courage, Enthusiasm, Determination, Respect, Loyalty, Drama, Generous, Charismatic, Big Heart, Arrogant, Loud, Dramatic, Headstrong, Forthright, Dignity, Sincere, Playful, Fun, Noble, Confident.

Leo
Motivational Reminder
(July ♌ 21st - August 20th)

Out of my natural strength
grows greater confidence in my abilities.
I take pride in helping those around me.
By owning my power, I shine;

I am strong and fear nothing that can come to me.
I look conflict in the face and move forward.
I am big hearted and will not be troubled by trifles.
I move steadily towards my purpose,
calm of mind and cool of courage.

I lead, I am a shepherd not a sheep and I am successful.
Big ideas, big plans with plenty of scope,
I devour with enthusiasm.

The Lantern and the Tree

The **Lantern of Creativity** has a bright orange glow. This one shines more brightly than any of the others - it almost stands alone. This is the heart of creativity, the joy and laughter of a hot summer's day where basking in the sun brings a feeling of warmth and belonging. Look deep into the orange glow of Leo and see a hearth fire - watch as others are drawn to its contained yet consistent flames. This is the Lantern of Creativity and holds within it the key to self mastery.

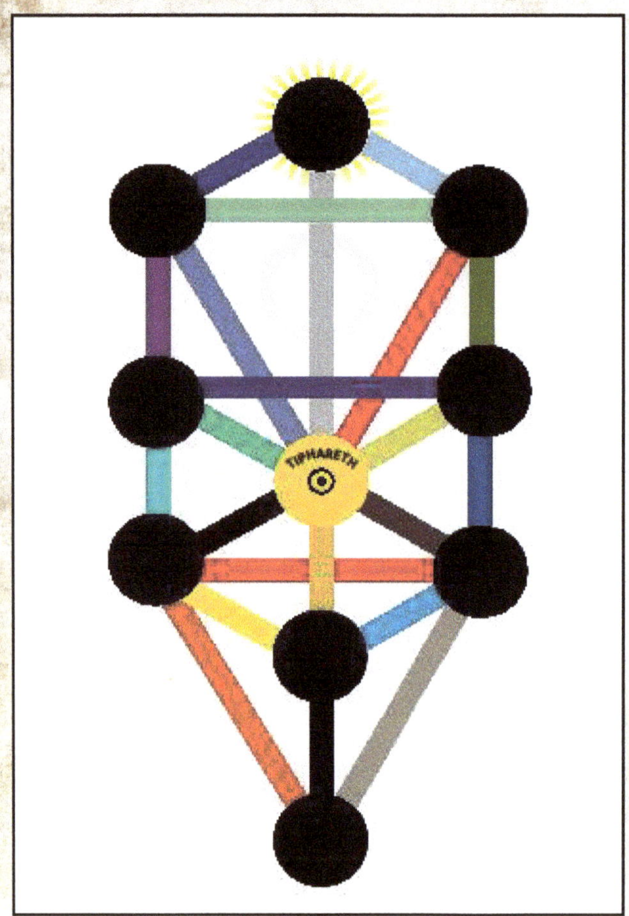

The Lantern of Creativity corresponds with the 6th sphere of Tiphareth, which is ruled by the sun - the same ruler of Leo. The sun is the heartbeat of our existence and represents our urge to live - to feel alive and be happy.

Here sits the Cosmic Law of Adaption. This sphere contains the keys to leadership of the self under the direction of the soul intention (higher self). Connecting to your own creative force and adapting to the flow of the universe.

If your sun sign is in Leo then your personality sphere on the Tree of Life is Tiphareth.

Virtue: **Devotion to the Great Work**
Vice: **False Pride**

Leo sits on the 19th pathworking on the Tree and aligns with the Strength/Lust tarot card.

Incense: **Frankincense**
Precious Stone: **Topaz, Yellow Diamond**

Exercises for Connection

The Lantern of Creativity is about knowing who you are and being ready to discover your potential, so that your light may shine as bright as the sun. It is the conscious effort you make in order to know who you are. There is no greater leader than the one who knows who he/she is and understands his/her own inner forces. Create the life or outcome that you wish by embracing your own creativity and uniqueness.

When one knows oneself and understands the inner forces, they do not seek to place blame on others, but instead take responsibility for themselves; using the inner furnace to light the Lantern and illuminate the path ahead. In doing so they also light the way for others, that they may find their own internal light and in turn do the same.

The Seven Questions of Leo

 In your journal, write down the answers to these questions to see how the Lantern of Creativity is working within your life.

1. How do you express your creative force?

2. When do you feel at your happiest?

3. Think of a time in your life where you felt you could really shine...

4. What makes you feel alive?

5. Do you enjoy playing games?

6. How playful are you?

7. When are you at your most confident?

Use this time to remember how to have fun and play - laughter lifts the spirit and warms the soul. Study an empowering art such as Qabalah that prepares the way for self-knowledge and discovery. Practice building up your own personal chi/prana by learning qigong, yoga, a martial art or t'ai chi.

Read the reminder to focus and align yourself with the essence of this time of year. If you were born in the sign of Leo, use the reminder as a realignment tool for your wellbeing.

Look at where Leo sits in your birth chart and the area of life it governs - where you express your creative force. Look to the Sun to see where you shine.

'You have power over your

own mind,

not outside events.

Realise this and you will

find strength.'

Marcus Aurelius

Lantern of Reason
The Heart of Virgo

"I Observe," Purity
Craftsman, Resourcer

☿

Ruled by Mercury
- Urge to serve

Sign: **Virgo**
Element: **Earth**
Force of Nature: **Mutable - Resourcer**
Planet Ruler: **Mercury**
Psychological Age: **Student**
Animal: **Ant/Bee/Virgin**

Archetype: **Craftsman**
House Position: **6th house**
Tool: **Disc of strength**
Time of Year: **Summer Finale**
Colour: **Olive**
Lantern: **Reason**

Welcome to the final phase of summer when Nature is preparing and adapting itself for autumn. The element is mutable earth. It is a time of harvest, when man reaps the rewards of all that he has sown earlier in the year. He works the fields and gathers his crops - they are his resources for the winter. Trees stand tall with their branches reaching for heaven, while the roots penetrate deep within the earth.

The virgin is the female associated with Virgo, indicating purity of mind. This is the mind that analyses, discerns and applies reason. She analyses the parts to understand the whole. Purity of mind subdues the negative part of the ego and there is a feeling of desire to serve her fellow man.

The psychological age of Virgo is the student - the quest for studying to attain knowledge in order to perfect techniques. This is the master craftsman. A person born at this time of year knows that if they prepare themselves adequately, they will find confidence in delivery and in turn be rewarded for their efforts. These are the hard workers with a flair for organisation and attention to details.

The mindset is in gaining knowledge to be of service to others - to assist others to be creative, apply reason and realise their potential. Intuitive reasoning brings synthesisation of all that has been gathered.

The Keywords of Virgo: Critical, Analytical, Practical, Commonsense, Reasoning, Details, Health, Methodical, Helpful, Reliable, Precise, Modest, Adaptable, Humility, Purity, Studious, Intelligent, Observation.

Virgo
Motivational Reminder
(August ♍ 21st – September 21st)

I know where my life is heading and I will not be swayed.
I bend with the winds of reason and
yet stay rooted to my course.
I do one thing at a time and each is done efficiently.
The seeds I am sowing are the seeds of development.
I know what I want and I am confident
I will reap the rewards.
My spirit is strong enough to meet all life's challenges.
I have a mental force that is powerful,
I concentrate easily and achieve whatever
I put my mind to.

By perfecting my techniques I become
a beacon for others.

The Lantern and the Tree

The **Lantern of Reason** is harder to see as it shines a muted glow of green - but if you concentrate and focus, you will see workers busy; look more closely and see the bees collecting pollen and then lower down, where the ants are working hard to take materials back to their nest.   The Lantern of Reason holds within it purity of mind and service.

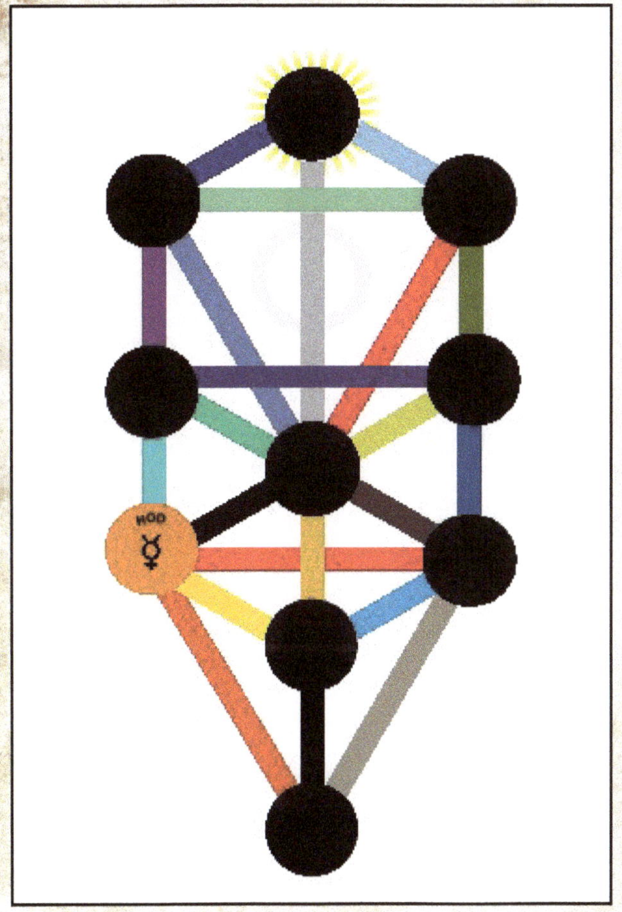

The Lantern of Reason corresponds with the 8th sphere of Hod, which is ruled by Mercury - the same ruler of Virgo. Mercury in Virgo is the quest to analyse and perfect techniques so they may be of service.

Here sits the Cosmic Law of Images (as in Gemini). This sphere also contains the seeds for spiritual purity manifesting on earth - reason becomes a tool that creates understanding. Words are chosen with care.

If your sun sign is in Virgo then your personality sphere on the Tree of Life is Hod.

Virtue: **Truthfulness**
Vice: **Falsehood, Dishonesty**

Virgo sits on the 20th pathworking on the Tree and aligns with the Hermit tarot card.

Incense: **Storax, Rosemary, Wisteria**
Precious Stone: **Opal, Citrine, Amber**

Exercises for Connection

The Lantern of Reason creates the perfect environment for studying and applying oneself to a subject. Perfecting one's potential becomes the focus, analysing and discerning between what is useful and what is not. As in Nature it is a time for the harvest, reaping what we have sown and sorting out the 'wheat from the chaff' - so it is in our lives.

The Seven Questions of Virgo

In your journal, write down the answers to these questions to see how the Lantern of Reason is working within your life.

1. In knowing who I am – what adjustments do I need to make, for others?

2. In knowing what I want – am I prepared to pay the price?

3. My attitude I understand – how does it help the options that are available to me?

4. In knowing where I come from – how does this limit me?

5. In knowing my potential – will it lead me to my objective?

6. So how do I perfect myself in order to overcome what worries me?

7. What routines can I introduce in my life that will make things easier?

Developing useful routines can make life easier, for instance, such as making your bed first thing in the morning when you get up. If your day has been long and hard and you are tired or you haven't been able to achieve anything else that day, you have achieved this. You will appreciate a ready bed all the more.

The mind is connected to the health of the body and this works both ways. Ask yourself if you are taking good care of your health needs... Are you due a check up?

Read the reminder to focus and align yourself with the essence of this time of year. If you were born in the sign of Virgo, use the reminder as a realignment tool for your wellbeing.

Look at where Virgo sits in your birth chart and the area of life it governs - where do you pay attention to the details? Look to Mercury to see how observant you are.

Summer Season
Famous persons born in Cancer, Leo, Virgo

Cardinal Water, Cancer
Nelson Mandela, Benedict Cumberbatch, Princess Diana, Prince William, Tom Cruise, Harrison Ford, Tom Hanks, Sylvester Stallone, Patrick Stewart, Richard Branson, Rembrandt, Julius Caesar, Ginger Rogers, Yul Brynner, Liv Tyler, Robin Williams, Travis Fimmel, Lindsay Lohan, Ariana Grande.

Fixed Fire, Leo
Barack Obama, Madonna, James Cameron, Ben Afflick, Nigel Mansell, Claudius I, George IV, Anna Kendrick, Antonio Banderas, Chris Hemsworth, Halle Berry, Robert De Niro, James Corden, Arnold Schwarzenegger, Jennifer Lopez, Nikolaj Coster-Waldau, Jason Momoa.

Mutable Earth, Virgo
Mother Teresa, Adam Sandler, Colin Firth, Hugh Grant, Keanu Reeves, Beyonce Knowles, Michael Keaton, Idris Elba, Michael Buble, Guy Ritchie, Jason Statham, Sam Neill, Sean Connery, Sophia Loren, Cameron Diaz, Stephen King, Agatha Christie, Freddie Mercury, Chris Pine, George R R Martin.

The Autumn Lanterns
Libra, Scorpio, Sagittarius

Lantern of Beauty
Libra, Cardinal Air

September 22nd – October 21st

Lantern of Regeneration
Scorpio, Fixed Water

October 22nd – November 21st

Lantern of Vision
Sagittarius, Mutable Fire

November 22nd – December 20th

Lantern of Beauty
The Heart of Libra

"I Relate," Equilibrium
Balancer, Initiator

♀
**Ruled by Venus
- Urge to love**

Sign: **Libra**
Element: **Air**
Force of Nature: **Cardinal - Initiator**
Planet Ruler: **Venus**
Psychological Age: **Young Adult**
Animal: **Dove/Scales**

Archetype: **Mediator/Balancer**
House Position: **7th house**
Tool: **Sword of peace**
Time of Year: **Autumn Equinox, Mabon**
Colour: **Pink**
Lantern: **Beauty**

It is the beginning of Autumn, when day equals night, the element of cardinal air. Beautiful honey-coloured golden leaves swirl around in gusts of wind.

Libra is represented by the scales, signifying balance, peace, intellectual harmony, equilibrium and justice, although equilibrium cannot be constantly maintained as change is a process of Nature. So it is with Libra, when the Libran's scales dip, they have to work hard within themselves to readjust back to a point of balance.

There is an urge to love, to write literature and poetry, to appreciate beauty and grace; to be surrounded by order and serenity brings peace of mind. This is the peacekeeper bringing objectivity, fairness and judgement - a mental champion who will stand up for the underdog.

The psychological age is that of a young adult reaching out to share his life with someone who will complement his nature. The self is no longer enough, so there is desire to reach out to another, to seek co-operation. A mental restlessness can be found here due to maintaining a constant balance between the heart and the head, between themselves and another and between thoughts and feelings.

The mindset of this time of year is in creating unity between all persons. This is the social innovator - bridging and fusing social gaps to bring balance and ease of communication to the world.   There is the perception of a common thread that links everyone.

The Keywords of Libra:
Peace, Adjustment, Equilibrium, Balance, Justice, Judgement, Objectivity, Love, Diplomatic, Compromise, Charming, Tactful, Sociable, Refined, Mediator, Artistic, Indecisive, Lazy.

Libra
Motivational Reminder
(September ♎ 22nd - October 21st)

My mind is balanced with my heart
in a state of equilibrium.
I am above petty prejudices and seek justice in all things.
I shall not allow fear to stop me from my purpose.
My mind seizes upon the fundamental points
and does not let them go.
I remain objective and without preconceptions.
I am unafraid of what others think and say.
Independent of mind
I can afford to be honest and objective.

I create unity, bridging and fusing social gaps.
I will leave this world better for my having entered it.

The Lantern and the Tree

The Lantern of Beauty has a pink glow, look into the lantern and really see the depth of its beauty.   A single rose appears perfect in shape and colour, now look beyond the rose and see the gusts of wind blowing the leaves into different places. You have to keep adjusting your focus to keep up with the sudden movements - art changes shape before your eyes, altering your perception of the images you are seeing. This is the Lantern of Beauty and holds within it the keys to unconditional love and our perception of truth and reality.

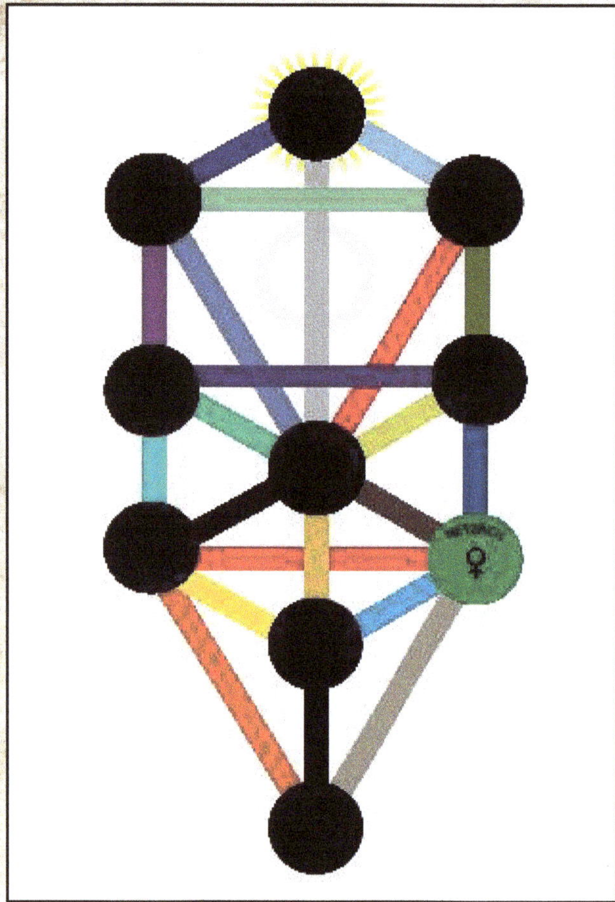

The Lantern of Beauty corresponds with the 7th sphere of Netzach which is ruled by Venus. Venus in Libra is our urge to love and share our lives with another.

Here sits the Cosmic Law of Perception (as in Taurus). The root of this sphere, from the perspective of Libra, is found in perceiving truth and understanding - the meaning of 'unconditional love.'

If your sun sign is in Libra then your personality sphere on the Tree of Life is Netzach.

Virtue: **Unselfishness**
Vice: **Lust for Power, Unchastity**

Libra sits on the 22nd pathworking on the Tree and aligns with the Justice/Adjustment tarot card.

 Incense: **Rose, Sandalwood, Benzoin**
Precious Stone: **Emerald, Malachite**

Exercises for Connection

The Lantern of Beauty seeks to reach out to another through our close relationships and determines how well we create balance in our lives. It can highlight how easy or difficult we find it to bring ourselves back to a point of equilibrium when our own internal scales tip.

The Seven Questions of Libra

In your journal, write down the answers to these questions to see how the Lantern of Beauty is working within your life.

1. Do you find it easy to compromise?

2. Are you scared of commitments?

3. Do you learn from others' experiences?

4. Do any qualities within your relationships reflect what you need in order to find balance within yourself?

5. Do your thoughts agree with your feelings?

6. In this moment - does your head align with your heart?

7. What type of person are you attracted to?

This time of the year the focus is upon finding the balance within - it could be an idea to explore body balancing techniques such as applied kinesiology, healing or meditation. Perhaps you are drawn to work with poetry, the arts, music, colours or sound?

Read the reminder to focus and align yourself with the essence of this time of year. If you were born in the sign of Libra, use the reminder as a realignment tool for your wellbeing.

Look at where Libra sits in your birth chart and the area of life it governs - where do you seek to compromise? Look to Venus to see how you express your feelings.

'Do not pray for an easy life,

pray for the strength to endure
a difficult one.'

Bruce Lee

Lantern of Regeneration
The Heart of Scorpio

"I Desire," Transformation
Investigator, Stabiliser

♇
Ruled by Pluto
- Urge to transform

Sign: **Scorpio**
Element: **Water**
Force of Nature: **Fixed - Stabiliser**
Planet Ruler: **Pluto**
Psychological Age: **Lover**
Animal: **Scorpion/Eagle**

Archetype: **Investigator**
House Position: **8th house**
Tool: **Cup of love**
Time of Year: **Samhain, 15° Scorpio**
Colour: **Purple**
Lantern: **Regeneration**

Autumn is fully established and has taken hold. This is the element of fixed water represented by the iceberg that contains beneath its surface a larger mass than appears above. Or we can liken it to a still, deep pond hiding its secrets within. Nothing is as it seems - there is always some depth of emotion contained and concealed behind the outer appearance.

There are two creatures associated with Scorpio - the scorpion and the eagle. The eagle can soar to the heights and fly directly into the eye of a setting sun then swoop down with accuracy and speed to swiftly kill its prey. The scorpion's natural instinct is to hide, scuttling away to the safety of the darkest of corners, making it difficult to see. The sting of a scorpion's tail is painful to receive but when the scorpion is trapped or cornered, it will turn on itself and commit suicide.

The psychological age is that of the lover - deeply sexual, with intense emotions, jealousy, passion and explosions. Looking to explore deeper feelings and unlock the hidden emotions that lie within. This is the master of disguise, the detective.

The mindset of this time of year is an intense, penetrating, magnetic, resilient, powerful and yet mysterious one that can keep its own secrets guarded and yet you will feel compelled to disclose yours. Scorpio seeks to transform. Out of the ashes of his desires he is resurrected as the phoenix, aflame with an inner brilliance and tremendous healing ability to lighten the core of any problem.

The Keywords of Scorpio:
Transformation, Intense, Magnetic, Willpower, Deep Feelings, Perceptive, Healing, Determined, Observant, Resilient, Passionate, Detective, Investigative, Secretive, Loyal, Focused, Mysterious, Revenge, Jealousy.

Scorpio
Motivational Reminder
(October ♏ 22nd - November 21st)

I have immense power flowing through my veins.
My will is strong and enduring.
Once I set my course, through unswerving dedication
and desire, I am never distracted from that path.
Caution protects me and I operate wisely.

I choose to state facts clearly with tact
and a kind deliverance.
Scheming and arguing unsettle my emotions.

Through transmutation of my emotions,
I rise empowered, having the might to help others,
and I will.

The Lantern and the Tree

The Lantern of Regeneration looms ahead, you pause, take a deep breath and look into the flame of Scorpio. The image of an eagle slowly comes into focus; flying in the sky, circling its prey. A second eagle flies in the direction of the west and looks straight into the eye of the setting sun. The vision fades and an iceberg reveals itself, with only one tenth of its true size showing above the water. The Lantern of Regeneration holds within it the keys to our own power, the mysteries revealed.

The Lantern of Regeneration corresponds with the 5th sphere of Geburah, which is ruled by Mars, the same ruler as Aries but not the natural ruler of Scorpio. Pluto its natural ruler sits in Daath, which is a gateway, a portal and not used as a sphere, therefore the original ruler of Scorpio, Mars is aligned instead. Mars in Scorpio is our urge to transform ourselves so that we function in harmony with our conscience.

The Cosmic Law of Karma reminds us of the consequences of our actions. The sphere contains within it the root of power, the greater mysteries and empowerment.

If your sun sign is in Scorpio then your personality sphere on the Tree of Life is Geburah.

Virtue: **Energy, Courage**
Vice: **Cruelty, Destruction**

Scorpio sits on the 24th pathworking on the Tree and aligns with the Death tarot card.

Incense: **Tobacco, Basil, Copal, Cinnamon**
Precious Stone: **Ruby, Garnet**

Exercises for Connection

The Lantern of Regeneration is magnetic and intense. It is where we delve to find out what is hidden beneath the surface and identify its root cause. From this knowledge - transformation, perception changing and deep healing can take place. The still waters of Scorpio run deep.

The Seven Questions of Scorpio

In your journal, write down the answers to these questions to see how the Lantern of Regeneration is working within your life.

1. Ask yourself, is there some issue that has been smouldering away within?

2. How do you adapt and cope with intense situations?

3. How do you handle pain?

4. When you feel emotional - what do you do?

5. Which is the easiest and hardest to handle – physical, emotional or mental pain?

6. How do you conserve your inner power?

7. Do others entrust their secrets to you?

Many people do not realise that when we are emotional it is not the time to confront our emotions. Instead, in the moment, write your thoughts and emotions in a journal, then go for a walk to clear your head or find someone you trust to talk to and get it out in the open. This will release the pressure that is building up inside. The pressure of the emotions is released via the physical, mental and spiritual levels.

Read the reminder to focus and align yourself with the essence of this time of year. If you were born in the sign of Scorpio, use the reminder as a realignment tool for your wellbeing.

Look at where Scorpio sits in your birth chart and the area of life it governs - where you seek to investigate and delve deeper. Look to Pluto to see how and where you transform.

Lantern of Vision
The Heart of Sagittarius

**"I Discover," Adventure
Explorer, Resourcer**

**Ruled by Jupiter
- Urge to grow**

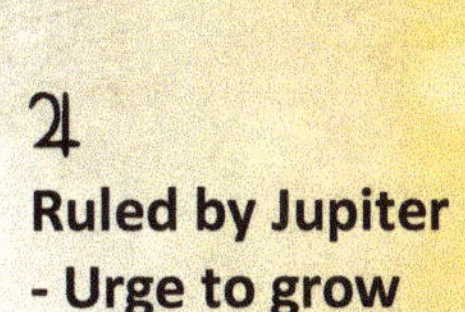

Sign: **Sagittarius**
Element: **Fire**
Force of Nature: **Mutable - Resourcer**
Planet Ruler: **Jupiter**
Psychological Age: **Adult**
Animal: **Centaur/Horse**

Archetype: **Explorer**
House Position: **9th house**
Tool: **Wand of courage**
Time of the Year: **Autumn Finale**
Colour: **Maroon**
Lantern: **Vision**

Nature is adapting ready to embrace the winter months ahead.   This is the element of mutable fire, the burning of grasses and refuse in the last of autumn days. Uncontained, wild fire, which will sometimes burn itself out and other times will spread quickly, consuming all in its path.

The centaur is associated with Sagittarius. Half man and half horse, he holds his arrow pointed aloft to the sky towards wisdom and understanding. His arrow is always fixated upon his ultimate goal, his ideal vision and the bigger picture. The horse referred to is the mustang - the wild, untameable free spirit.

The psychological age is that of an adult and the mind turns towards philosophical, cultural or higher learning activities in order to expand awareness and grow. Travel is his passion - taking risks or taking a chance is all part of the game. Happy-go-lucky, laid-back, intellectual and very forgiving, enthusiastic to the core and slightly over the top.

This is the mindset of the spontaneous adventurer, the sportsman, the free spirit who is enthusiastic and optimistic. His quest is his life - this is his spiritual search for the Holy Grail. The teacher who has not only knowledge but also experience, so that he may teach and enrich humanity.

The Keywords of Sagittarius:
Visionary, Quest, Goals, Idealistic, Enthusiastic, Optimistic, Adventurous, Free Spirit, Indulgent, Laid-back, Spontaneous, Opportunity, Expansion, Honest, Forgiving, OTT, Exaggerate, Sporty, Good Humour.

Sagittarius
Motivational Reminder
(November ♐ 22nd - December 20th)

With pure motive, joy and a good heart I go forward
to conquer my goals and reach my ideals.
Strong of enthusiasm and spirit, I shall not falter.
My amiable character allows me to take
the rough with the smooth.
Even when I am competing, I give others a fair chance.

I have confidence and optimism in myself and in the world.
With my boundless energy I concentrate on my target,
focus my mind and hold my course.

I make my goals and visions a reality.

The Lantern and the Tree

The **Lantern of Vision** has flames that are wild, untamed and random, shedding a spectacular dance of light on the pathway in front of us. Looking deeper into the lantern we see a mustang horse, wild and untamed. He meets our gaze; it feels as if his eyes can see directly into our hearts. He turns and gallops off into the horizon. This is the Lantern of Vision containing within it the seeds of hope and the great masterpiece of our life's mosaic.

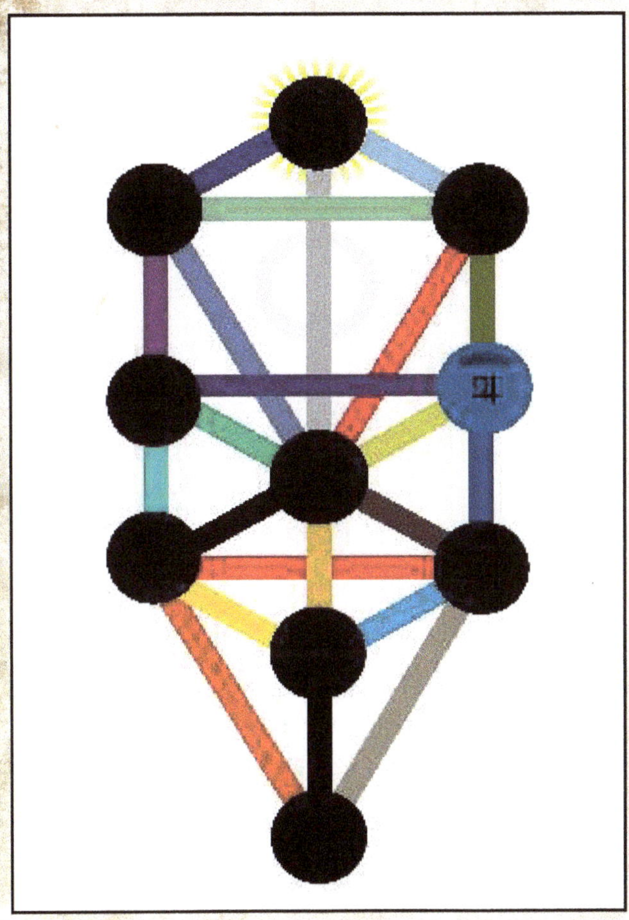

The Lantern of Vision corresponds with the 4th sphere of Chesed, which is ruled by Jupiter, the same ruler as Sagittarius. Jupiter is our urge to discover and grow - broadening our minds and horizons with exploration.

The Cosmic Law of Order and Timing aligns with Chesed showing us everything has its time and place. This sphere contains the essence of hope - it is the vision of the bigger picture, the Great Masterpiece, the Spiritual Mosaic.

If your sun sign is in Sagittarius then your personality sphere on the Tree of Life is Chesed.

Virtue: **Obedience**
Vice: **Hypocrisy, Gluttony, Bigotry**

Sagittarius sits on the 25th pathworking on the Tree and aligns with the Temperance/Art tarot card.

Incense: **Cedar, Nutmeg, Thyme**
Precious Stone: **Sapphire, Lapis Lazuli**

Exercises for Connection

The Lantern of Vision is open to new experiences, determined to make the best of life, forthright and sociable, seeking adventures, expanding the mind and spiritual growth. This lantern opens you up to exploring different avenues to seek a higher meaning to life.

The Seven Questions of Sagittarius

In your journal, write down the answers to these questions to see how the Lantern of Vision is working within your life.

1. Are you a pessimist or an optimist?

2. How does your outlook affect your life choices?

3. Do you find it easy to be spontaneous?

4. Do you seize the day?

5. How open are you to a new adventure?

6. Name your current goals in life...

7. How quick are you to accept a challenge?

Study the works of the great philosophers. Start to write down your daily contemplations either first thing or before you go to bed. This unravels the thoughts and clears the mind ready for the day or night ahead, giving you insights into the depths of your own thinking and reasoning, allowing your subconscious mind the space to communicate to you.

Read the reminder to focus and align yourself with the essence of this time of year. If you were born in the sign of Sagittarius, use the reminder as a realignment tool for your wellbeing.

Look at where Sagittarius sits in your birth chart and the area of life it governs - where do you likely take risks and seek an adventure? Look to Jupiter to discover inner growth and expansion.

'In order to carry a positive

action we must develop

here a positive vision.'

The Dalai Lama

Autumn Season
Famous persons born in Libra, Scorpio, Sagittarius

Cardinal Air, Libra
Oscar Wilde, Margaret Thatcher, Jimmy Carter, Julie Andrews, Sting, St Francis of Assisi, Charlton Heston, Jackie Collins, Kate Winslet, Sigourney Weaver, Matt Damon, John Lennon, Sharon Osbourne, Pavarotti, Roger Moore, Ralph Lauren, Jean Claude Van Damme, Lena Headey.

Fixed Water, Scorpio
Pablo Picasso, Leonardo DiCaprio, Martin Scorsese, Bill Gates, David Schwimmer, Dolph Lundgren, Matthew McConaughey, Bryan Adams, Art Garfunkel, Demi Moore, Julia Roberts, Ryan Gosling, Gerard Butler, Whoopi Goldberg, Owen Wilson, Meg Ryan, Anne Hathaway.

Mutable Fire, Sagittarius
Walt Disney, Steven Spielberg, Brad Pitt, Judi Dench, Jane Austen, Samuel L Jackson, Woody Allen, Bette Midler, Britney Spears, Ozzy Osbourne, Jeff Bridges, Kirk Douglas, Jamie Foxx, Theo James, Christina Aguilera, Scarlett Johansson, Jane Fonda, Kristofer Hivju.

The Winter Lanterns
Capricorn, Aquarius, Pisces

Lantern of Self-discipline
Capricorn, Cardinal Earth

December 21st – January 20th

Lantern of Freedom
Aquarius, Fixed Air

January 21st – February 19th

Lantern of Imagination
Pisces, Mutable Water

February 20th – March 20th

Lantern of Self-discipline
The Heart of Capricorn

"I Use," Boundaries
Manager, Initiator

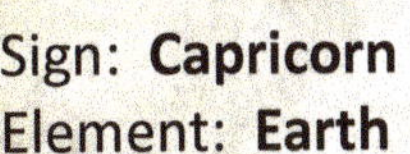

♄
Ruled by Saturn
- Urge to control

Sign: **Capricorn**
Element: **Earth**
Force of Nature: **Cardinal - Initiator**
Planet Ruler: **Saturn**
Psychological Age: **Middle Age**
Animal: **Goat**

Archetype: **Manager**
House Position: **10th house**
Tool: **Disc of strength**
Time of Year: **Winter Solstice, Yule**
Colour: **Black**
Lantern: **Self-discipline**

On the Winter Solstice, 21st December, the sun moves into Capricorn. Capricorn is the element of cardinal earth. This month contains the force of initiatory energy within it - the cold dryness of winter - when nature is active but hidden. Capricorn conserves this energy with care and discipline, beneath ground, within the depths of the soil.

The animal associated with January is the mountain goat. He climbs surefooted to the top of the ridge where he can see all around him and gain the overview. In making the sacrifice of leaving the green pasture he climbs to the safety of the heights.

We can liken this to a middle-aged person who has got to the peak of his career and will do what is needed to maintain his security, status and position. Responsibility and duty rest easily upon his shoulders whilst maintaining a cool, calm and collected demeanour. He likes to keep control, to respect tradition and strives to have a structure in place, while keeping an eye on those who have yet to make the climb.

The mindset of this month is very much like playing a game of chess - you need to keep your eye on the goal, while looking behind and to each side of you in order to anticipate another player's move, all the time weighing up all the options.

The Keywords of Capricorn:
Responsibility, Initiation, Ambition, Careful, Cautious, Very Serious, Limitation, Disciplined, Structure, Plan, Stability, Wise, Sure-footed, Calm, Cool, Calculated, Practical, Tradition, Manipulative, Inadequate, Control, Restrictive.

Capricorn
Motivational Reminder
(December ♑ 21st - January 20th)

My life is well planned
and in all things I use a proven structure.
New ideas are welcome; I assess their value
and incorporate them into my routine.
I do my duty with enjoyment and fulfilment.

Every day I climb higher up the ladder towards the peak.
I stand firm on loyalty, honesty and fairness.
I keep a cool head, I am cautious until I calculate the risk.
The greater the difficulties, the more heartily I attack them.

I seek to serve my generation ambitiously
with the tools that have been given to me.

The Lantern and the Tree

The Lantern of Self-discipline is very dim, there is hardly any light at all - just a strange halo. It appears as if this lantern is absorbing all the light around it - we stare into it and wait until the black turns to grey, revealing an image. Rocks are forming; lava is pushing its way up to the surface, breaking the earth's crust, pressure. Heat and force are combining to create the earth upon which we walk. This is the Lantern of Self-discipline. It is dealing with a pressure and force so powerful to wield that it requires self-discipline in order to create form - herein lie the keys to this lantern.

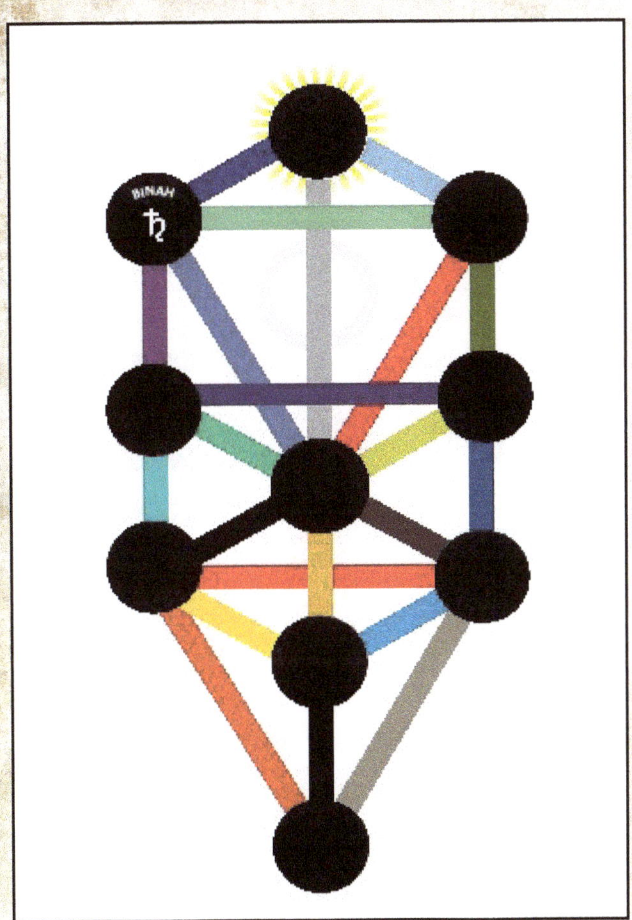

The Lantern of Self-discipline corresponds with the 3rd sphere of Binah, which is ruled by Saturn, the same ruler as Capricorn. Saturn is our urge to control and set boundaries in our life for our wellbeing.

The Cosmic Law of Polarity aligns with Binah, reminding us that opposites have the power to compliment each other. This sphere contains within it the seeds of faith found in the womb of the cave of silence.

If your sun sign is in Capricorn then your personality sphere on the Tree of Life is Binah.

Virtue: **Silence**
Vice: **Materialism, Avarice**

Capricorn sits on the 26th pathworking on the Tree and aligns with the Devil tarot card.

Incense: **Myrrh, Eucalyptus, Chamomile**
Precious Stone: **Obsidian, Onyx, Tourmaline**

Exercises for Connection

The Lantern of Self-Discipline gives us the energy to plan for the year ahead, to ensure security and stability, whilst taking into account duties and responsibilities.

Many start the year with a resolution, a new health regime or structure that they want to accomplish. Applying self-discipline, limiting our options - assists us by strengthening our will, conserving what we have, focusing on the now and concentrating on the task at hand.

The Seven Questions of Capricorn

In your journal, write down the answers to these questions to see how the Lantern of Self-discipline is working within your life.

1. Do you have a plan for the coming year?

2. Do you find yourself blaming others instead of taking responsibility?

3. How disciplined are you in life?

4. How important are traditions to you?

5. Do you know your own limits?

6. How easy is it for you to create healthy boundaries?

7. How easily are you distracted?

Capricorn aligns with our National Karma, here is where you apply discipline to your life in order to take responsibility for your actions; realising the effect that you have on others. To increase your powers of observation and enhance your awareness of the process of cause and effect - play a game of chess or strategy.

The Lantern of Self-Discipline contains within it the seeds of faith, the cave of silence, and is the place of the Cosmic Mother. It is often asked why the colour black sits here - black absorbs all light - that is why a person who is feeling 'grief' will wear black as it assists us in absorbing as much light as possible, when we feel low allowing us to reconnect with our own light.

Read the affirmation to focus and align yourself with the essence of this time of year. If you were born in the sign of Capricorn, use the reminder as a realignment tool for your wellbeing.

Look at where Capricorn sits in your birth chart and the area of life it governs - where traditions and boundaries are important. Look to Saturn to learn how your urge to control expresses itself.

Lantern of Freedom
The Heart of Aquarius

"I Know," Intuition
Inventor, Stabiliser

♒

Ruled by Uranus
- Urge to change

Sign: **Aquarius**
Element: **Air**
Force of Nature: **Fixed - Stabiliser**
Planet Ruler: **Uranus**
Psychological Age: **Retirement**
Animal: **Peacock/Water Bearer**

Archetype: **Inventor/Humanitarian**
House Position: **11th house**
Tool: **Sword of peace**
Time of the Year: **Imbolc, 15° Aquarius**
Colour: **Turquoise**
Lantern: **Freedom**

The second month of winter has taken a determined and stabilising hold over the landscape. Aquarius is the element of fixed air, icy cold winds which can chill to the core and freeze over the stark terrain.

Man is associated with Aquarius and his quest for knowledge. He seeks unconditional love and truth that is crystal-clear clarity in its reasoning. Cold, hard facts, with sudden stark realisations and emotional objectivity, awaken intuition. This is represented by a water bearer that pours knowledge freely upon the earth keeping one foot on the ground (stability) and another in the water (feelings).

This is likened to the time in life when you have left the cycle of work and are retired. Through maturity, the stabilisation of the emotions allows for the lightning rod of truth to strike, ideas abound and traditions and structures that are no longer useful or harmful are challenged. Humanity, the origin of existence, global awareness, cosmology and science all awaken the consciousness.

The mindset of this month is a quest for truth and enlightenment, to rise above personal prejudices and pre-conditioning, giving an individual the independence and freedom to serve humanity in the way that aligns with their unique destiny.

The Keywords of Aquarius:
Genius, Ideas, Electric, Cosmos, Independent, Bizarre, Truth, Unique, Original, Ice Cold, Shocking, Humanitarian, Honest, Eccentric, Unconventional, Strong Willed, Rebellious, Scientific, Chaotic, Freedom, Intuition.

Aquarius
Motivational Reminder
(January ♒ 21st - February19th)

I am determined that all my thinking processes
shall be in a state of order.
My mind is open to receive, ideas are generated,
I share to the benefit of others.

I speak the truth with honesty and clarity,
aware of others' sensitivity and I deliver this with tact.
I rise above arguing and being pedantic;
I do the right thing.
I let my intuition guide me.
I radiate sympathy and good feeling.

To serve humanity is my chief aim.

The Lantern and the Tree

The Lantern of Freedom has a turquoise glow. As we gaze into it we see a peacock with an array of beautiful feathers, strutting and displaying himself in full glory. As he moves away a man appears; he has one foot on the earth and the other in the water. He is holding a container of water that he pours freely upon the ground - his contribution to creation. With all the elements in play a rainbow appears behind him. This is the Lantern of Freedom and holds the seeds of originality and the key to being true to oneself.

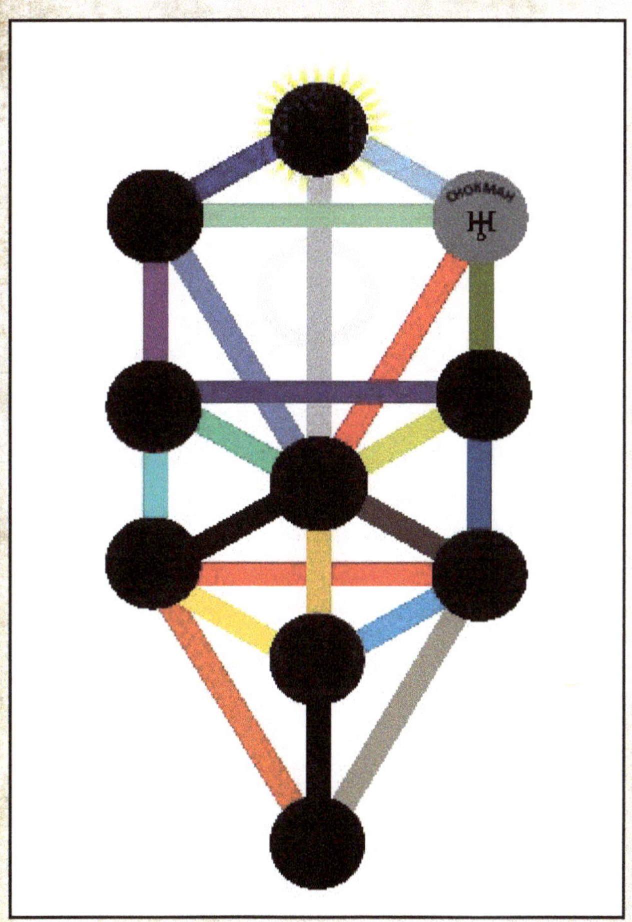

The Lantern of Freedom corresponds with the 2nd sphere, Chokmah. Ruled by Uranus, it has the same ruler as Aquarius. Uranus is our urge to change and our lives are continually changing. Its essence is our acceptance of change once the old ways no longer serve our needs.

The Cosmic Law of Rotation aligns with Chokmah, reminding us of the cycles that are operating around and within. This sphere contains the force behind our creativity and originality. It is the key to turning our knowledge into wisdom.

If your sun sign is in Aquarius then your personality sphere on the Tree of Life is Chokmah.

Virtue: **Devotion**
Vice: **Chaos**

Aquarius sits on the 28th pathworking on the Tree and aligns with the Star tarot card.

Incense: **Musk, Sage**
Precious Stone: **Turquoise, Chrysocolla**

Exercises for Connection

"Happiness and freedom begin with a clear understanding of one principle: Some things are within our control, and some things are not. It is only after you have faced up to this fundamental rule and learned to distinguish between what you can and can't control that inner tranquillity and outer effectiveness become possible." Epictetus (AD c. 55-135)

The Lantern of Freedom encourages us to 'think outside the box' and look at the world through a different lens. It asks us to 'shake off the shackles' and make the changes necessary, so that we may live our lives in accordance with our truth - no matter how bizarre that life appears to others. Freedom finds its strength in uniqueness and a little non-conformity balances the pressure to follow the crowd.

The Seven Questions of Aquarius

In your journal, write down the answers to these questions to see how the Lantern of Freedom is working within your life.

1. What does freedom mean for you?

2. How do you deal with unexpected changes?

3. Is it easy for you to be objective?

4. How easy is it for you to be independent?

5. In a group situation, what part do you play?

6. Do you have more close friends or more acquaintances?

7. How easy is it for you to network?

To get the best out of this time of year, concentrate on developing your intuition and crystallising your intelligence by stimulating and engaging the mind. Brainstorm ideas with others. Follow the trends in science. Study or watch cosmology programmes to activate the enquiring mind. Join a study group and engage with others on a subject that interests you; champion a humanitarian issue that may pull you towards others of a like mind.

Use the affirmation to focus and align yourself with the essence of the time of year. If you were born in the sign of Aquarius, use the motivational reminder as a realignment tool for your wellbeing.

Look at where Aquarius sits in your birth chart and the area of life it governs - where do you take an unconventional approach? Look to the position of Uranus to see how you handle change.

'Observe the movements of the stars as if you were running their courses with them, and let your mind constantly dwell on the changes of the elements into each other.'

Marcus Aurelius

Lantern of Imagination
The Heart of Pisces

"I Believe," Dreams
Healer, Resourcer

Ψ
Ruled by Neptune
- Urge to Dream

Sign: **Pisces**
Element: **Water**
Force of Nature: **Mutable - Resourcer**
Planet Ruler: **Neptune**
Psychological Age: **Old Age**
Animal: **Salmon/Two fishes/Dolphin**

Archetype: **Healer**
House Position: **12th house**
Tool: **Cup of love**
Time of Year: **Winter Finale**
Colour: **Violet/Deep sea blue**
Lantern: **Imagination**

The last phase of winter sees the dissolution and slow withdrawal of the cold as the sun ascends toward the new equinox. Nature prepares itself for the rebirth of a new season. Pisces is the element of mutable water - we can imagine this as waves crashing onto the shore, wild seas and high tides disguising the stillness on the sea bed.

The salmon is associated with Pisces. Salmon adapt to their environment by migrating to the sea but when it is time to spawn to reproduce life, they show great strength by swimming upstream against the current.

We have reached the psychological time of old age when a slow withdrawal from the outer world makes room for a greater inner world. At this point the veil between astral and the physical worlds is thin. It is a highly sensitive and fragile time when the dream world interchanges with the real or manifested world. Deep emotions ebb and flow from within, moving freely back and forth from one dimension to the next. Strength and wisdom are drawn from memories kept close to the heart, embracing faith, hope and charity through a compassionate desire to help others.

The mindset of this time of year is one of compassion and sensitivity to all living things. It transforms dreams and ideals into reality through using the imagination to light the beacon of charity. It is the belief that miracles can really happen and is the builder of dreams.

The Keywords of Pisces:
Highly Sensitive, Psychic, Imagination, Sacrifice, Dreams, Adaptable, Emotional, Gentle, Healing, Fearful, Compassionate, Escapism, Devotion, Impressionable, Elusive, Nebulous, Cantankerous.

Pisces
Motivational Reminder
(February ♓ 20th - March 20th)

Ideals and dreams stem from the depths of my being
and I express these in my daily actions.
I analyse my thoughts and use a methodical process
to bring structure to my imaginative mind.

My smile is infectious and spreads joy to others.
I believe in the charitable nature of the human race
and this encourages me to make this world
a place of greater happiness.

Through my unswerving faith and empathic awareness
I demonstrate hope for mankind.

The Lantern and the Tree

The Lantern of Imagination looks older than the others, but although it is aged, it has not lost any of its power. We look into this sign and see a shimmering veil of sparkling silver that pulls itself back to reveal an image of our dreams. Eventually the image fades and we hear waves crashing upon the shore. This is the Lantern of the Imagination – the end of a cycle and yet the beginning of a new one awaits. It contains the keys to the fount of all things in the universe.

The Lantern of Imagination corresponds with the 1st sphere of Kether which is ruled by Neptune, the same ruler as Pisces. Neptune is our urge to dream and to imagine.

The Cosmic Law of Expression aligns with Kether, reminding us of our creative potential, to express ourselves and shine. This sphere contains within it the fount of all things in the universe - it is the alpha and the omega, the beginning and the end.

If your sun sign is in Pisces then your personality sphere on the Tree of Life is Kether.

Virtue: **Attainment, completion of the great work (the union of spirit, soul and personality)**
Vice: **Divisiveness**

Pisces sits on the 29th pathworking on the Tree and aligns with the Moon tarot card.

Incense: **Ambergris, Almond**
Precious Stone: **Diamond**

Exercises for Connection

The Lantern of Imagination has a strong connection to the astral worlds and the subconscious mind. Having a conscious recollection of our dreams can give us an insight into what our subconscious is telling us.

The Seven Questions of Pisces

In your journal, write down the answers to these questions to see how the Lantern of Imagination is working within your life.

1. Do you remember your dreams? How easy are they to recall?

2. Write up the last few dreams you remember and make a conscious effort to do this every day.

3. What rocks your boat?

4. Is there a fear within that is getting in the way of happiness?

5. What sacrifices are you making right now?

6. How vivid is your imagination - do you have an inner fantasy world?

7. How sensitive are you?

The more sensitive and aware we become of others and our environment, the easier it is to take on negative energies. Learn how to protect your energy, take time out for you, a place of sanctuary to recharge. You can cleanse your aura and alleviate aches and tension by taking a bath with a spoon of Epsom salts in it. Sea salt is an alternative.

The Lantern of Imagination is the oldest lantern and contains all the experience of the other eleven within it. It is assimilating, merging, dissolving and unifying the parts into a whole.

Read the affirmation to focus and align yourself with the essence of the time of year. If you were born in the sign of Pisces, use the reminder as a realignment tool for your wellbeing.

Look at where Pisces sits in your birth chart and the area of life it governs - where do you express your sensitive side? Look to the position of Neptune to understand your urge to dream.

Winter Season
Famous persons born in Capricorn, Aquarius, Pisces

Cardinal Earth, Capricorn
Mohammed Ali, George Foreman, Joe Frazier, J Edgar Hoover, J R R Tolkien, A A Milne, Joan of Arc, Elvis Presley, Martin Luther King, Al Capone, Cary Grant, Kevin Costner, Mel Gibson, Nicholas Cage, Jim Carrey, Anthony Hopkins, Denzel Washington, Rod Stewart, Kit Harrington.

Fixed Air, Aquarius
Charles Dickens, Abraham Lincoln, Charles Darwin, George Washington, Ronald Reagan, Mozart, James Dean, Morgan Fairchild, Clark Gable, Alice Cooper, Jennifer Aniston, Jerry Springer, Jane Seymour, John McEnroe, Paris Hilton, Yoko Ono, John Travolta, Galileo.

Mutable Water, Pisces
Michelangelo, Albert Einstein, Glenn Miller, George Washington, Ron Howard, Mikhail Gorbachev, Karen Carpenter, Jon Bon Jovi, Chuck Norris, Jessica Biel, Liza Minnelli, Michael Caine, Eva Longoria, Nat King Cole, Bruce Willis, Adam Levine, Justin Bieber, Sophie Turner, Rihanna.

12 Shining Lantern
Pathworking Visualisation

Pathworking

Journey in your mind through the 12 Lanterns to contemplate their meaning and to ask them to reveal their special message to you.

1. Light a candle and some incense, sandalwood or woody tones.
2. Sit in a comfortable position, preferably facing the east. The east marks the point of the beginning - the sun rises in the east. Most religions traditionally build their altars facing this direction.
3. Read through the whole detailed visualisation first and then you may begin the journey in your mind.
4. When you have read through the visualisation below, close your eyes and in your mind walk the pathway. Start at the forest with the path in front of you, go to each lantern in turn until you reach the old oak tree. Pick a Lantern to work with, then place it on the branch. On your return, take note of the lanterns as you walk back to the forest entrance.
5. After completing this visualisation, consolidate by writing down all that you can remember - the things you saw and heard - as this is helpful for memory recall. You can also cross check prominent colours or images with the correspondences for each sign to gain further insight.
6. Bring your awareness back down to earth by grounding yourself. Have something to eat and drink - this will help with grounding.

Detailed Visualisation

We are going to take a journey to the temple forest, so sit comfortably with your feet firmly on the ground. Imagine a golden light surrounding you as you enter the temple Forest, a familiar woodland space. Take time to digest your surroundings.   In front of you a pathway is lit by 12 lanterns. At the end of the pathway, in the distance you can see a large oak tree, with a comforting light shining from an entrance at the base of the trunk.

You feel compelled to take this well-lit path and you approach the first lantern. It is a single flickering golden flame - the beginning, birth and the spark of creation. Look deeper into the flame and the image of a warrior is revealed, full of energy, heightened survival instinct and ready for action. This is the Lantern of Energy and holds within it the key to our own energy.

Continuing along the path, the second lantern is shining a light green consistent glow, lighting up the next segment. Look deeper into the flame and you see a fertile field, resplendent with red poppies - a contented bull full of strength and static solidity, stares back at you. This bull is at home with familiar things; he likes to be comfortable within his environment as consistency sustains his nature. This is the Lantern of Strength and holds the key to our own core and internal strength.

We continue to the third Lantern of Gemini and are welcomed by a bright yellow light dancing and flitting around. Looking deeper into the lantern we see tiny sylphs - the elemental beings of air - hovering and playing, dancing in the soft warm breeze. Butterflies flit from one brightly coloured flower to another.   This is the Lantern of Language and holds the key to our attitude and communication.

The fourth lantern now beckons and this has a silvery glow shining onto the path. As you gaze into the lantern you see a bright summer's day with a cascade of fresh, cleansing, pure water as it descends from the mountains in the north. These are waters of life, reflection and memory, nurturing and nourishing the earth so that we may have a foundation of growth. This is the Lantern of Nurturing and holds the key to our root foundations.

The bright orange glow of the fifth lantern now catches our eye. This one shines more brightly than any of the others - it almost stands alone. This is the heart of creativity, the joy and laughter of a hot summer's day where basking in the sun brings a feeling of warmth and belonging. Look deep into the orange glow of Leo and see a hearth fire – watch as others are drawn to its contained yet consistent flames. This is the Lantern of Creativity and holds within it the key to self mastery.

We know we must continue the path and move on to the sixth lantern. This lantern has a smoky green muted glow and is harder to see into but if you concentrate and focus, you will see workers busy; look closely and see the bees collecting pollen and then lower down, where the ants are working hard to take materials back to their nest.   This is the Lantern of Reason and holds within it purity of mind and service.

We approach the pink glow of the seventh lantern. Look into the lantern and really see the depth of its beauty.   A single rose appears perfect in shape and colour, now look beyond the rose and see the gusts of wind blowing the leaves into different places. You have to keep adjusting your focus to keep up with the sudden movements - art changes shape before your eyes, altering your perception of the images you are seeing. This is the Lantern of Beauty and holds within it the keys to unconditional love and our perception of truth and reality.

The pink glow fades into purple as we move towards the eighth lantern on the pathworking.   You stop, hesitate and take a deep breath before looking into the flame of Scorpio, the lantern of regeneration. The image of an eagle slowly comes into focus; flying in the sky, circling its prey. A second eagle flies in the direction of the west and looks straight into the eye of the setting sun. The vision fades and an iceberg reveals itself, with only one tenth of its true size showing above the water. The Lantern of Regeneration holds within it the seeds of knowledge and the keys to our own power, the mysteries revealed.

The ninth lantern is bright before us and we notice its flames are wild, untamed and random, shedding a spectacular dance of light on the pathway. Looking deeper into the lantern we see a mustang horse, wild and untamed. He meets our gaze; it feels as if his eyes can see directly into our hearts. He turns and gallops off into the horizon. This is the Lantern of Vision containing within it the seeds of hope and the great masterpiece of our life's mosaic.

We leave this bright uplifting light and head towards the 10th lantern, noticing that there is hardly any light at all - just a strange halo. It appears as if this lantern is absorbing all the light around it - we stare into it and wait until the black turns to grey, revealing an image. Rocks are forming; lava is pushing its way up to the surface and breaking the earth's crust, pressure. Heat and force are combining to create the earth upon which we walk. This is the Lantern of Self-discipline. It is dealing with a pressure and force so powerful to wield that it requires self-discipline in order to create form - herein lie the keys to this lantern of Capricorn.

The oak tree is coming into focus now at the end of the pathway. We approach the 11th Lantern - it has a turquoise glow and as we gaze into it, we see a peacock with an array of beautiful feathers, strutting and displaying himself in full glory. As he walks away a man appears; he has one foot on the earth and the other in the water. He is holding a container of water that he pours freely upon the earth - his contribution to creation . With all the elements in play a rainbow appears behind him. This is the Lantern of Freedom and holds the seeds of originality and the key to being true to oneself.

At last we complete our journey and arrive at the violet glow of the 12th Lantern. This lantern looks older than the others. Although it is aged, it has not lost any of its power. As we look into the lantern we see a shimmering veil of sparkling silver that pulls itself back to reveal an image of our dreams. Eventually the image fades and we hear waves crashing upon the shore. This is the Lantern of the Imagination - the end of a cycle and yet the beginning of a new one awaits. It contains the seeds of the fount of all things in the universe.

The golden light in the doorway of the old oak tree looks welcoming and inviting in front of us. We walk towards the tree and see the 12 lanterns now hanging on the tree on the lower branches - which one are you attracted to? Take your chosen lantern off the tree, sit down and look deep into the light. What is its message for you?

When you are finished, hang the lantern back on the tree and walk along the pathway. Note as you pass whether any of the lanterns look different now.   Back at the entrance to the temple forest, you bring your awareness back to your body and the here and now.

Section Three
Glossary

How to read an Ephemeris

The chart below is an example page taken from an Ephemeris.   An Ephemeris is used to calculate where the sun and other planets sit at the time of your birth. If you are born on the cusp of a sign you can find out the exact time and date that the sun enters the sign for the year of your birth.

Look to the column that contains the Sun symbol ☉ you will note that on the first day of the month, labelled Day 1, the sun is in Pisces - 10°45. Look further down the column and on Day 21 the sun changes and enters Aries. The next column is the moon and on Day 1 it is in Aries; on Day 3 it has moved into Taurus. So if you were born on 6th March, your sun would be in Pisces and your moon would be in Gemini. The sun represents our true nature, our urge to live and what we need from life in order to feel alive and be happy. The moon represents our emotional reactions, habits and responses.

March 2017 — Tropical Midnight Ephemeris — Time Zone: EDT (04:00 West)

Day	☉	☽	+12 Hr ☽	True ☊	☿	♀	♂	♃	♄	♅	♆	♇
1 W	10 ♓ 45 23	13 ♈ 34 42	20 ♈ 40 28	03 ♍ 22 R	05 ♓ 43 D	12 ♈ 56 D	23 ♈ 34 D	22 ♎ 19 R	26 ♐ 44 D	22 ♈ 06 D	11 ♓ 40 D	18 ♑ 46 D
2 Th	11 45 37	27 47 48	04 ♉ 56 11	03 21	07 32	13 02	24 18	22 15	26 47	22 08	11 42	18 48
3 F	12 45 48	12 ♉ 05 08	19 14 09	03 20	09 22	13 07	25 01	22 10	26 50	22 11	11 45	18 49
4 Sa	13 45 58	26 22 50	03 ♊ 30 46	03 19	11 14	13 08	25 45	22 06	26 54	22 14	11 47	18 50
5 Su	14 46 06	10 ♊ 37 36	17 43 04	03 19	13 06	13 08 R	26 28	22 01	26 57	22 17	11 49	18 52
6 M	15 46 11	24 46 52	01 ♋ 48 48	03 19 D	15 00	13 04	27 12	21 56	27 00	22 20	11 52	18 53
7 Tu	16 46 15	08 ♋ 48 40	15 46 16	03 20	16 54	12 59	27 56	21 51	27 03	22 23	11 54	18 54
8 W	17 46 16	22 41 29	29 34 09	03 21	18 49	12 50	28 39	21 46	27 06	22 26	11 56	18 55
9 Th	18 46 15	06 ♌ 24 08	13 ♌ 11 19	03 22	20 45	12 40	29 22	21 40	27 08	22 29	11 58	18 57
10 F	19 46 12	19 55 33	26 36 43	03 23	22 42	12 26	00 ♉ 06	21 35	27 11	22 32	12 01	18 58
11 Sa	20 46 06	03 ♍ 14 44	09 ♍ 49 27	03 23	24 39	12 11	00 49	21 29	27 14	22 35	12 03	18 59
12 Su	21 45 59	16 20 50	22 48 47	03 23 R	26 37	11 52	01 32	21 24	27 16	22 38	12 05	19 00
13 M	22 45 50	29 13 16	05 ♎ 34 18	03 21	28 35	11 32	02 16	21 18	27 19	22 41	12 07	19 01
14 Tu	23 45 39	11 ♎ 51 54	18 06 10	03 19	00 ♈ 33	11 09	02 59	21 12	27 21	22 44	12 10	19 02
15 W	24 45 26	24 17 13	00 ♏ 25 14	03 16	02 32	10 44	03 42	21 06	27 23	22 47	12 12	19 04
16 Th	25 45 11	06 ♏ 30 28	12 33 11	03 12	04 30	10 17	04 25	20 59	27 25	22 50	12 14	19 05
17 F	26 44 54	18 33 45	24 32 31	03 09	06 28	09 48	05 08	20 53	27 27	22 53	12 16	19 06
18 Sa	27 44 36	00 ♐ 29 57	06 ♐ 26 30	03 05	08 24	09 17	05 51	20 46	27 29	22 56	12 19	19 07
19 Su	28 44 16	12 22 42	18 19 04	03 03	10 20	08 44	06 34	20 40	27 31	23 00	12 21	19 08
20 M	29 43 54	24 16 10	00 ♑ 14 37	03 01	12 14	08 10	07 17	20 33	27 33	23 03	12 23	19 09
21 Tu	00 ♈ 43 30	06 ♑ 15 00	12 17 57	03 01 D	14 06	07 35	08 00	20 26	27 34	23 06	12 25	19 09
22 W	01 43 05	18 24 02	24 33 51	03 02	15 56	06 59	08 43	20 19	27 36	23 09	12 27	19 10
23 Th	02 42 38	00 ♒ 47 57	07 ♒ 06 51	03 04	17 42	06 22	09 25	20 12	27 37	23 12	12 29	19 11
24 F	03 42 09	13 30 59	20 00 45	03 06	19 26	05 44	10 08	20 05	27 39	23 16	12 32	19 12
25 Sa	04 41 38	26 36 25	03 ♓ 18 10	03 07	21 06	05 07	10 51	19 58	27 40	23 19	12 34	19 13
26 Su	05 41 06	10 ♓ 06 03	16 59 59	03 07 R	22 41	04 29	11 34	19 51	27 41	23 22	12 36	19 14
27 M	06 40 31	23 59 45	01 ♈ 04 58	03 05	24 12	03 51	12 16	19 44	27 42	23 26	12 38	19 14
28 Tu	07 39 55	08 ♈ 15 05	15 29 27	03 02	25 38	03 14	12 59	19 36	27 43	23 29	12 40	19 15
29 W	08 39 16	22 47 15	00 ♉ 07 37	02 57	26 59	02 38	13 41	19 29	27 44	23 32	12 42	19 16
30 Th	09 38 35	07 ♉ 29 35	14 52 11	02 52	28 14	02 03	14 24	19 21	27 45	23 36	12 44	19 16
31 F	10 37 53	22 14 28	29 35 31	02 46	29 23	01 29	15 06	19 14	27 45	23 39	12 46	19 17
1 Sa	11 37 08	06 ♊ 54 33	14 ♊ 10 50	02 41	00 ♉ 26	00 56	15 49	19 06	27 46	23 42	12 49	19 18

Reference Guide to Symbols

Point of Spring Equinox – Aries
The symbol of Aries is drawn like the horns of the ram.

30 degrees removed from Spring Equinox – Taurus
The symbol of Taurus is the nose ring of the bull.

60 degrees removed from Spring Equinox – Gemini
The symbol of Gemini is two lines the same, like twins,
but joined top and bottom.

**90 degree angle from the point of Spring Equinox and the
beginning of Summer Solstice – Cancer**
Drawn as a sideways 69, cancer represents the breast.

120 degrees removed from the point of Spring Equinox – Leo
The symbol of Leo is drawn like a lion's tail.

150 degrees removed from the point of Spring Equinox – Virgo
The symbol of Virgo is similar to MD; we can remember this as
medical doctor, as Virgos are concerned with health.

**180 degrees removed from the point of Spring Equinox and the
beginning of the Autumn Equinox – Libra**
The symbol of Libra is drawn like a bridge in a road, or a pair of scales.

210 degrees removed from the point of the Spring Equinox – Scorpio
The symbol of Scorpio is drawn as an M for mystery with a scorpion's tail.

240 degrees removed from the point of the Spring Equinox – Sagittarius
The symbol of Sagittarius is the arrow of the centaur.

270 degrees removed from the point of the Spring Equinox – Capricorn
The symbol for Capricorn is drawn as a VS; we can remember this
by the words 'very serious.'

300 degrees removed from the point of the Spring Equinox – Aquarius
The symbol for Aquarius is drawn as two wavy lines; we can remember
this as two waves of electricity.

330 degrees removed from the point of the Spring Equinox – Pisces
The symbol for Pisces is the letter H with curvy lines; we can
remember this as two fish in opposite directions but joined together.

The Lights

The Symbol for the sun is a circle with a dot in the centre. This can
be likened to the sun being the centre of the solar system, or as the nucleus of
a cell. Meaning: Urge to live.

The symbol for the moon is drawn when it is in its waxing mode as the
moon is moving from the New Moon to the full moon, this is when the
moon is illuminated on the right. Meaning: Urge to respond.

The Planets

The symbol for mercury is a combination of the circle, the semi-circle and the cross
of matter; representing the force of intelligence. Meaning: Urge to communicate.

Venus combines the circle over the cross of matter; representing the idea of 'as in
heaven, so on earth.' Meaning: Urge to love.

Mars is the reverse of Venus with the cross of matter at the end in the direction of
an arrow; representing base desires. Meaning: Urge to survive.

Jupiter is drawn like a back to front j, he is composed of the semi-circle and the cross
of matter; representing wisdom. Meaning: Urge to grow.

Saturn is drawn similar to the letter h. It is composed of the semi-circle and the cross
of matter; representing the material world. Meaning: Urge to control.

The symbol for Uranus could be likened to an aerial. It is comprised of a semi-circle
placed on either side of the cross, over a small circle; representing enlightenment.
Meaning: Urge to change.

Neptune is drawn like Neptune's trident in mythology. Is the semi-circle pierced by
the cross of matter; representing sensitivity. Meaning: Urge to dream.

Pluto is drawn as a P after Percy Lowell whose calculations led to the discovery
of Pluto 14 years after his death; representing death and rebirth.
Meaning: Urge to transform.

The Lanterns and
Emotional Freedom Technique (EFT)

The Lanterns can be used by Healers and Practitioners. The following is a guide to using the Lanterns as an information tool to bring balance back to the emotional body. This guide uses the top line emotion from the Behavioural Barometer *(by Three in One Concepts.)*

The Lantern affinity has been added to the chart as a way of balancing the negative words to which the body is reacting.

Acceptance **Antagonism**

Lantern of Language
Gemini, light energy, air, intellect, I think.
Seeking to spread the word.

Willing **Anger**

Lantern of Self Discipline
Capricorn, dense energy, earth, practical, I use.
Seeking to master the self.

Interest **Resentment**

Lanterns of Transformation and Nurturing
Scorpio, Cancer, stagnant energy to cleansing energy, water, feelings, I desire and feel.
Seeking to awaken.

Enthusiasm **Hostility**

Lantern of Vision
Sagittarius, wild untamed energy, fire, action, I see.
Seeking the unknown.

Assurance **Fear of Loss**

Lanterns of Energy and Creativity
Aries, Leo, first spark of energy to the steady consistent force, fire, action, I am and I lead.
Seeking to be a leader of oneself.

Equality **Grief and Guilt**

Lantern of Beauty
Libra, balanced healing energy, air, intellect, I balance.
Seeking to love.

Attunement	Indifference	**Lantern of Freedom** Aquarius, lightning bolt of energy, air, intellect, I know. Seeking enlightenment.
Oneness	Separation	**Lantern of Imagination** Pisces, universal consciousness, flowing energy, water, feelings, I believe. Seeking unity
Choice	No Choice	**Lanterns of Strength and Reason** Taurus, Virgo, stable contented energy, earth, practical, I want and I examine. Seeking security and clarity.

When a sign/lantern is stressed, the reactions/emotions are found in the opposing sign. In order to create balance work on both.

LANTERN	⟷	LANTERN
Energy ♈	Balance Point	Beauty ♎
Strength ♉		Regeneration ♏
Language ♊		Vision ♐
Nurturing ♋		Self-Discipline ♑
Creativity ♌		Freedom ♒
Reason ♍		Imagination ♓

Further Reading

Linda Goodman, *Linda Goodman's Sun Signs: The secrets of astrology revealed for every single sign of the zodiac*, Pan Books Ltd, 1968.

Julia and Derek Parker, *Parkers' Astrology*, Dorling Kindersley, 1991.

Marcus Aurelius*, Meditations*, Penguin Classics, 1995.

Ryan Holiday, *The Ego is the Enemy*, Portfolio; 1 edition (June 14, 2016).

David Wells, *Qabalah: Discover powerful tools to explore practical magic and the Tree of Life*, Hay House UK, 2017.

Gareth Knight, *A Practical Guide to Qabalistic Symbolism*: Volumes I and II, Kahn & Averill, 1965.

"I wish you joy in working with the Astrological Wheel of the Year and the template of 12 Lanterns that provide a framework to access your inner compass. We all go through periods of peace and adversity and it is helpful to have tools that aid us, enabling us to maintain a balanced, informed view of situations. Becoming more familiar with Astrology and Stoic Qabalah reminds us of who we are, what we want, what is important in our lives and why we are here. Using the lanterns enables us to connect with our essence and keep our minds elevated, amidst the daily struggles which affect us all.

Everyone has the ability to light their own beacon and in turn light their own path. The knowledge to attain this state of clarity is no longer for the few but for the many. We are entering the age of Aquarius. Aquarius rules Astrology and the 'Way of the Sun'- there has never been a more poignant time. This knowledge can serve as a lifelong toolbox, opening the doors to all hidden knowledge as well as the adventure and mysteries of man's being."

Cathy Stronach - *Qualified 1996 – The MAAT Order, Portsmouth, UK*
M.A. Astro.Dip. - A Honours www.cathystronach.com
Member of Astrological Association of Great Britain